CALHOUN AREA WRITERS
Telling Stories 2

ISBN-13: 978-1986758772

ISBN-10: 198675877X

A portion of the proceeds from the sale of this book is being given to Ferst Foundation For Childhood Literacy. Ferst is a nonprofit with the mission to provide books for local communities to prepare children, beginning at birth, for reading and learning success.

You can learn more about Ferst and how to get involved by visiting their website.

http://ferstreaders.org/

Our Authors

Karli Land
Amber Lanier Nagle
Vickie McEntire
Millicent Flake
Brian Grogan
Kay Whatley
Gene Magnicheri
Janette Stephenson
Mike Ragland
Cheryll Snow
Marla Aycock
Gordon Flowers
Mandy L Cantrell
DB Martin
Michael Zemaitis
Jan Deems

To the members of the Calhoun Area Writers.

In 2014, I looked for a few writing friends. I called us the Calhoun Area Writers. Who knew where we would be just four short years later. The success of this group is because of its members. I am grateful to each and every one of you for what you contribute, not just to CAW but to my life. It is an honor to call you my friends.

-Karli Land

Karli Land

Calhoun Area Writers Founder & President

Frostproof, Florida native, Karli Land, resides in Calhoun, Georgia with her husband, four children, and a grand baby. She is the founding president of the Calhoun Area Writers and the Northwest Georgia Writers Conference, and is the Young Adult Services Coordinator for the Calhoun-Gordon County Library.

Karli enjoys writing children's picture books, middle-grade fiction, and Christian non-fiction. She currently has two works-in-progress, *Day After Yesterday*, a novel following the life of a daughter as she fills the role of caretaker to her mother suffering from Alzheimer's Disease and *The Others*, a Christian Bible study written for women serving in ministry.

She has freelanced for the *Calhoun Times, Calhoun Magazine, Fort Meade Daily News* and has had several articles published in e-zines and online journals.

She is the author of *Baby, Don't Cry, Made to Move* and the blog *Too Hot To Be A Grandma*.

Journaling Through Motherhood
Karli Land

My journal entry from January 31, 1999

All packed up and ready to leave the hospital, the nurse stops me at the door, arms outstretched, handing me my new baby. I have to take it home???

Until this moment, through months of pregnancy, setting up a nursery, and buying lots and lots of baby supplies, it hadn't dawned on me what was about to happen. Not only would I take this baby home with me that day, I would also be carrying home all the emotions that come along when the life and well-being of another human falls on your shoulders. You are faced with decisions about things you hadn't really thought important until that moment. Decisions about health, nutrition, which pediatrician you should use, what schools are the best, what sports are the safest, and which neighborhood should you live in. And moms have a terrible habit of looking to others to set the standard of what is the norm. In our social-media driven society, it is hard to watch other moms posting their best mommy-moments and not feel like you come up a little short. I want to step up to say, I am in the same boat as you. Anything you've done, anywhere you've fallen short, I can honestly say "me too!" I've fed my kids Doritos straight out of the bag and called it dinner. I've had to loan my son a pair of my fuzzy socks because I was behind on laundry. We have skipped bath time because we spent time in the pool so the kids are probably clean enough. I've sent my kids to bed early because I have a bag of mini donuts hidden in the back of the pantry that I would like to enjoy alone.

We all have those moments we would rather others not know anything about. And what do we do? We clean up those messes and take a photo shopped selfie with our kids so that everyone else thinks we are as perfect as they want us to think they are. It's a vicious cycle mommas. We've got to stop the comparing and let go of the guilt. No mommy is a perfect mommy.

Several years ago I found myself in a mommy-pit. After months of complete bedrest, I had just given birth to our fourth child. She was a preemie, spent time in the NICU, and went home on a heart monitor. She required much attention and took up a lot of my time. Meanwhile, I had three other little ones who were homeschooled and needing me to focus. Aside from all the baby care, I spent my mornings teaching, my afternoons planning lessons, and my nights crying to my husband because I felt like each day was a failure. I was sure that my children would one day be in a therapy session crying their way through a suppressed memory about how I had failed to cut the crust off of their peanut butter sandwich. The final straw came when I let my middle daughter's birthday slip up on me, leaving me totally unprepared for her big day. I found myself hyperventilating on the party aisle of a nearby dollar store trying to put together a party setup from the mismatched items they had available. We lived too far from town and I had too little time to put together anything great so with a little desperation and a lot of shame, I called all of our closest friends and begged them to come over for a party that should have been planned months earlier. I baked a half-burnt cake and smeared on some pink icing. With an unsteady hand, I did my best to write Happy Birthday Princess on the top and used small toys lying around the house for cake toppers. We did have balloons but couldn't find streamers so we used household items like tin foil and toilet paper to make the house look festive. A few folks showed up, gift-less because of the last minute invite, but instead sympathetically handed her some cash. We played some games that didn't require preparation and after a round of the birthday song, we allowed our guests to leave. It was officially the worst birthday party ever given and that meant I was the worst mommy to ever exist. I sat in our living room that night and I cried. I just knew that I had scarred my child for life and that she would one day leave my home, never looking back. I walked the hall to her bedroom to tell her I was sorry for being such a terrible mother when I heard her talking to her sister. "Today was the best day ever. Maybe you can have a party like mine when it's your birthday."

The lesson to take away from this is simple. We might not have it all together but our kids don't know that. They think that the moon hangs in the sky because we put it there. And that is exactly what we do. We hang their moon. We make them proud. We love them like there's no tomorrow and they give us their utmost loyalty and refuse to let a negative thought about us cross their minds. They put us on a pedestal but being a mommy is hard work and we deserve that pedestal. So stand tall momma, knowing that your circumstances are different from any other mother's and you only have to do your best. Whether you are the mom of girls or the mom of boys, the mom of a special needs child or an empty nest mom, you are the most important person in your child's life. You might not have all the laundry done and only clean in the main parts of the house on a regular basis but you spend time with your babies and they think you're great.

Now, wipe the powdered sugar off your chin and turn your shirt right side out cause you've got a moon to hang.

My journal entry from April 27, 2016

My heart is full as I watch my four beautiful children walk side-by-side through life. I have so much more than I deserve. I pray for joy in the midst of trials because no matter what I am going through, I always have my kids to look forward to.

Other Journal Entries (just for kicks):

April 8, 2000

Note to self: If you leave a baby near your sweep pile, they will turn it into an all-you-can-eat buffet.

June 19, 2012

First clue that my kiddo is not ready to potty train...when I opened her new potty seat, she got so excited ....then put it on her head like a hat.

August 17, 2012

I'm going to start wearing a big purple suit to teach my kids. I tell them to turn the water off while they're brushing their teeth to save water, I get nothing. Barney throws it into a song and all of a sudden they're water conservation experts!

August 14, 2010

Just wiped down with a baby wipe and called it a shower. Is it wrong? Probably, but I'm just too tired to care.

August 29, 2010

Caught my oven on fire trying to sneak in a late night snack...tried to stay calm so the kids wouldn't notice but jumping up and down in the kitchen screaming, "What do I do, what do I do?" got them out of bed.

September 2, 2010

Totally just sent all my kids in to clean their rooms so that I could have the trampoline all to myself.

Walks With Memaw
Karli Land

The sun starts to make its way into the western sky, leaving in the clouds behind it the most radiant shades of red and orange. Dark is coming which only motivates me to clear my dinner plate faster knowing that I won't be excused from the table until I do. After I get the okay from momma, I jump up from my seat and run full force through the house and out of the front door causing the screen door to slam closed behind me. Dad shouts a warning, "don't slam the door," but I don't even look back. I make my way across the driveway and over into the next yard. Outside, my papaw is watering his well-kept rose bushes and manicured lawn. He lifts the water hose my way, pretending that he is going to soak me with it but I know better from the many times we've played this game before. I make my way through his yard and up to the house. I sling open the front door and yell inside. "We goin today?" I wait to hear the small, sweet voice of the woman who makes my world turn. I know she's in the kitchen, finishing up the dinner dishes but I don't dare step inside with my shoes on. "Almost ready," I hear my memaw call out.

It doesn't take much to keep a six-year-old girl from Frostproof, Florida entertained. We head down the driveway together and start out on our mile-long walk which consists of walking the streets of our neighborhood, Overocker Circle, four times. I don't remember the days before our walks started, in my mind it's just what we've always done. I don't think that it was the walks that I enjoyed but rather the games that were played along the way. We sang nursery rhymes, played I-spy, told stories and talked about our day. Walks around that little country block is where I was first introduced to Baa, Baa Black Sheep, The Three Bears, and Henny Penny. I heard my very first Dr. Seuss and Roald Dahl with sweaty palms and tired feet after a few times around the circle. I listened to made-up stories and configured my very own tall tales. Those moments were without a doubt where I first formed my love of words. I loved every word that came out of her mouth and now wish so much to have the opportunity to hear them all over again. As I memorized the songs and stories that she would teach me, I immediately began teaching them to my little sister. I just knew that she would need to know them one day for her walks with memaw. As our walks got fewer and fewer, we began taking along a notebook full of our little rhymes and I only recently realized its purpose. My memaw was losing her memories. My little sister would never enjoy the long walks and playful songs with our memaw. Alzheimer's took that opportunity away before she was old enough to even understand what was happening.

I write every day of my life now. Oftentimes I think of my memaw while I do knowing that she would be proud of me following my dreams. I am so grateful for the time that I had with her and the writer that I have become because of that time. I wouldn't trade it for anything in the world. I keep my own notebook now that I will one day share with my grandchildren as we hurry through our dinner plates, rushing outside to meet for our walks.

His Grace Is Sufficient
Karli Land

Ephesians 2:8-10 NIV

For it is by grace you have been saved, through faith—and this is not from yourselves, it is the gift of God— not by works, so that no one can boast. For we are God's handiwork, created in Christ Jesus to do good works, which God prepared in advance for us to do.

I love to write. Most evenings you can find me in a corner somewhere with a laptop or a pen and a notebook. God has allowed me many great opportunities to write and share lessons that I have learned from His Word. There is something about writing a devotion or speaking to a group of ladies that fills my heart as I draw close to my Savior and listen to His voice telling me what we will do next. I know that I want to use the talents that God has given me to further His kingdom, but I clearly understand that those talents aren't what is getting me there. This is a lesson that took me many years to learn.

I accepted Christ when I was 15. At that time, I did not know what that meant for my life. I changed my friends and learned how to read God's Word. I attended church and involved myself in ministries that gave me the opportunity to serve. I tried my best to earn my salvation and I continued this for many years. It wasn't until just a few years ago that I understood God's grace. To any outsider, it would have appeared that I was at a peak in my life. I had an amazing and supportive husband, was enjoying a peaceful life in the mountains of Northwest Georgia, had many Christ-loving, spirit-led friends and had just given birth to my fourth child. But in the midst of all of that outward perfection came a battle that I had fought for years. I struggled with my worth as a person; as a wife, mother, friend, Christian. It was a battle that I could no longer fight.

In Deuteronomy chapter one, Israel refused to enter into the Promised Land. God had led His people out of bondage and despair and had given them a place to rest and restore. They were scared and lacked faith. Verse 28 says that they cried out "The people are greater and taller than we." This was my cry. I couldn't compare to the mothers who kept perfect houses and led Scout meetings. I wasn't like the wives that I knew- the ones that packed lunches for their hubbies and never spoke an angry word. My life was filled with so many spiritual giants that I didn't think that God would even be able to see me standing behind them trying to earn His love by singing in the choir and teaching a Sunday school class. I couldn't measure up and claim my promised land because I wasn't good enough. I couldn't fight that battle.

Verse 30 and 31 says, "The Lord your God, who goes before you, He will fight for you, according to all He did for you in Egypt before your eyes and in the wilderness where you saw how the Lord your God carried you, as a man carries his son, in all the way that you went until you came to this place."

You see sisters, my battle was not with other Christians. It wasn't against my friends or other moms. My battle was against my own doubts and insecurities. And my God says He will fight. He loves His children and He will fight their battles and when you think that you can't go any further, God will scoop you up into His loving arms and He will carry you. That, my friend, is grace.

Amber Lanier Nagle

Calhoun Area Writers Vice President

Amber Lanier Nagle came to the writing world a little later in life than most folks. She was thirty-six when she first picked up a pen and started writing short essays about her family, memories, and assorted experiences.

"Writing killed two birds with one stone," she says. "It allowed me to record and share the rich history of my family in a rather whimsical way, and more importantly, I found it to be an immensely therapeutic activity after losing my job that year. Writing helped me think through issues, and afterwards, I felt lighter and happier. That's how I got started."

Today, Amber is a freelance writer with hundreds of nonfiction articles in her portfolio. She's crafted both quirky human interest articles and detailed instructional features for *GEORGIA Magazine, GRIT, Points North, Mother Earth News, Natural Awakenings*, and so many others. From snakes to vintage trains to Christmas tree farms to hip replacement to financial advice to nuclear power to the elusive Bigfoot—she's written about nearly everything under the sun.

She is also the editor of *Calhoun Magazine* and *Health, Mind & Body Magazine,* glossy, bi-monthly magazines spotlight interesting people, places, and events in the Northwest Georgia region.

She pens a weekly column titled, "From the Porch" for the *Vidalia Advance* in South Georgia featuring articles about memories, relationships, and Southern potpourri. For example, she's written about chickens, boiled peanuts, bluebirds, crayons and coloring, Christmases past, stargazing, flat cornbread, the death of loved ones in her column.

She judged the essay collection entries for the 2017 Georgia Author of the Year awards.

She is the brainchild behind *Project Keepsake* (www.ProjectKeepsake.com*)*, an uplifting paperback collection of stories told in first-person by ordinary people about their treasured keepsakes and mementos. It was released in 2014 by Native Ink Press. It's available on Amazon, other online booksellers, a few brick-and-mortar locations, and at her events.

She also offers two eBooks online. *Southern Exposure* is a selection of twenty-two nonfiction articles perviously published in the *Calhoun Times* and inspired by her Southern upbringing. *Have a Seat* is a short instructional booklet with photos about caning chair seats using split reed.

Amber is currently slogging through her first novel, something she describes as both painful and infuriating. She hopes to complete the first draft of *Thirty Wooded Acres* by the end of

2018.

She's a dedicated writing coach who teaches memoir writing and freelancing workshops throughout the Southeast. And she has a blog (www.AmberNagle.com) where she offers posts about the writing process and the sometimes joyous, sometimes frustrating business of writing.

Amber holds technical degrees from Georgia Tech and Mercer University. She's a member of the Chattanooga Writers Guild, Georgia Writers Association, and Calhoun Area Writers.

She writes from her home in the woods in Northwest Georgia.

Death in the South
Amber Lanier Nagle

Mrs. Gump: "I'm dying, Forrest. Come on in, sit down over here."

Forrest Gump: "Why are you dying, Mama?"

Mrs. Gump: "It's my time. It's just my time. Oh now... don't you be afraid, sweetheart. Death is just a part of life."

--From Forrest Gump 1994

I rose early that day faced with the long, four-hour drive down to my stepfather's home in Southeast Georgia. I suppressed my many melancholy feelings by singing along to the radio and focusing my attention on each milestone along my journey— Atlanta's downtown connector, Hartsfield-Jackson International Airport, the large outlet mall in Locust Grove, Rose Hill Cemetery along the banks of the muddy Ocmulgee, and the point where the brown dirt on the sides of I-16 transitions to the white sand hills abundant in the lowland areas of Georgia.

"Which shoes should I wear?" Mom asked just moments after I arrived. She had hung her funeral attire on the door of the spare bedroom with two pairs of black pumps parked underneath.

"I don't know. Maybe those," I said pointing to one pair.

She agreed with my decision and dressed as I washed down a pack of cheese crackers with an ice-cold Coke. A half hour later, I was behind the wheel again, but this time, I chauffeured two others—Mom in the backseat and my stepfather riding shotgun in the front with me.

Freshly plowed dirt roads. Live oaks draped with cascading Spanish moss. Weathered clapboard houses. Barns strangled by tangles of kudzu. Fans of saw palmetto. Towering longleaf pines.

The three of us arrived at the funeral home in Richmond Hill and entered the building. Dozens of relatives—some I had not seen in over a decade—ambushed us. We mingled, hugged, waved, dried tears and pressed our way through a sea of grieving people to the open casket. My cousin, Yancey, dressed in a navy blue fisherman's shirt, lay peacefully before us as if he were taking a nap.

I stood next to my cousin's body and spoke to him with my thoughts.

I hate seeing you like this. I'll miss your wit—we all will.

I had not seen Yancey in a while, although he and I shared conversations and photographs via Facebook. He was my Aunt Joyce's youngest child—her baby boy, even at forty-seven years old. His rotund body seemed a perfect match for his larger-than-life personality, but his heart and his lungs couldn't support the surplus weight. Health problems plagued him at the end. His death was somewhat expected, but still, when my sister called and told me he had died, I was simply shocked. I gasped. News of death has that effect on me every time.

I hate saying goodbyes, and I've said a lot of goodbyes in my lifetime.

My Papa Lanier died of emphysema when I was seven, and I remember the weight of his death on my family and the pained, primitive yowls of my grandmother and my Aunt Colleen in the days that followed. They seemed inconsolable.

As a child, I also attended funerals for Uncle Lee Roy, Uncle Lewis, and many other relatives, and each time, Mom would escort me up to where the body rested and say, "You might want to look, Honey. It will be the last time you get to see him."

I didn't want to look, but I did. I saw death laid out before me—the lifeless, empty shells of people from my life. I witnessed the anguish of the survivors who occupied the front pews of the churches. I smelled the overpowering aroma of Chrysanthemums arranged in baskets and stuck in large, flashy sprays. I listened to the comforting messages of preachers guiding my imagination to images of winged souls flying up to Heaven. Unfortunately, I heard the other kind of sermons, too—the hellfire and damnation kind designed to terrify a congregation, wounded and weakened from loss.

"If you want to see him again, you must repent your sins and accept Jesus as your Savior *today*," some preachers howled while standing over the casket. "Only then can you be reunited with your loved ones in Heaven. Come to the front of the church *now* and reaffirm your faith. There may not be a tomorrow."

Friends and family members streamed forward. No one wanted to be left behind. No one wanted to spend eternity in Hell. *No one.*

Even as a little girl, I found the fire-and-brimstone sermons of some funerals distasteful. To me, the words "today could be your last chance for salvation," sounded a lot like a used car salesman's cheesy pitch—"What do I have to do to get you in this car today? It may not be here tomorrow. Better go ahead and buy it now."

My Grandmother Lanier died in 1990. My father wept for her.

My daddy joined Grandmother and Papa on the other side in 1992, and I cried for him *and* my mother who became a widow at fifty-five. We buried him in denim jeans and a flannel shirt because that's what he was most comfortable wearing. My father was a Mason, and so a band of Masonic brethren wearing white gloves and ceremonial aprons surrounded his body at the graveside. One man wore a hat and spoke directly to us.

"Our Brother has reached the end of his earthly toils. The brittle thread which bound him to earth has been severed and the liberated spirit has winged its flight to the unknown world. The dust has returned to the earth as it was, and the spirit has returned to God who gave it."

The service brimmed with poetic phrasing and symbolism— my kind of sermon. At one point, the man with the hat placed a sprig of cedar on my father's casket.

"This evergreen is an emblem of our enduring faith in the Immortality of the Soul. By it we are reminded that we have an imperishable part within us, which shall survive all earthly

21

existence, and which will never, never die. Through the loving goodness of our Supreme Grand Master, we may confidently hope that, like this Evergreen, our souls will hereafter flourish in eternal spring."

I loved the thought of my father existing in eternal springtime somewhere.

We buried my father that afternoon then went to a family member's house and ate. Women of the family and community had prepared a generous spread of fried chicken, chicken and dumplings, potato salad, cornbread, sweet tea, chocolate cake and other delicacies. Taking food to a grieving family is the epitome of Southern grace, like saying, "I'm sorry for your loss. I care. And don't ever forget—you are loved by so many."

After we picked at our food and rested for a while, my family caravanned back to the cemetery and stood beside the mounded dirt and flower arrangements for a few minutes. Mom reached down and plucked a limp rose from the spray that covered Daddy's grave—a keepsake she eventually dried and pressed between the pages of a Bible. We each selected a potted peace lily to take home.

I found it difficult to turn and leave my father at the cemetery that day. I believed his soul had moved on, yet I had a strong connection with the vessel that contained his being. I lingered at his graveside delaying the inevitable.

With its granite and marble obelisks and monuments, the cemetery looked a bit like an outdoor art garden. There was a strange beauty to the setting, although it was a barren land flush with death and sadness.

I drifted far away in thought.

When I was a little girl, Mom taught me cemetery etiquette.

"Walk on this side, Honey," she said, leading me around the headstones. "You don't want to walk over the 'person.' That's disrespectful. You wouldn't want anyone walking all over you, would you?"

From the time I could walk, I visited the cemetery to replace the artificial flowers at the headstones of family members. Some of the arrangements were faded and forgotten. When we would go to put out springtime flower arrangements, we'd take note of all the headstones that still had plastic Christmas poinsettias around the grave markers.

"Mama always hated to see Christmas arrangements out here at Easter," Mom said.

We'd survey and pull up any weeds littering one of our family's plots. Before leaving, we'd stroll through and study a few notable headstones.

Four graves were special because they had photos on the headstones.

"These people are my daddy's parents," she noted as we stood next to markers for Ed Lee Jarriel and Mary Catherine Cowart. We took a few steps over.

"And this is my Great Grandparents—your Great-Great Grandparents," she said as we stood at the stones of John L. Jarriel and Lucinda Kennedy. "Amber, look how thin Lucinda's hair was. That's where you and I get our stringy, sorry hair."

Then she chuckled. She went on to tell us stories about how John Jarriel and another family member had lost their arms—one in the Civil War and the other in a railroad accident.

"Think about how hard it was to work the land and raise farm animals with only one arm back then," she said. "But they did it. They didn't give up. They did what they had to do."

That was Mom's way of telling us that we come from a tough breed of people who push through hard times and persevere. She made a few final comments pointing to the men's eyes.

"Look at John's eyes. See how one squints a bit," she said. Then she stepped back to Ed Lee Jarriel's monument again. "Look at his eye—same squint."

I, too, have a 'squinting' eye. In almost every photo of myself, one eye is wide open and the other is slightly closed.

I drifted back into my body, but continued to stall by wading through the sea of headstones and reading the names, dates, and verses engraved on the surfaces. Finally, my husband grabbed my hand and led me away—back to the world of the living.

Since that day, I've lost others—my beloved Grandmother Jarriel, aunts, uncles, cousins, and friends. I've watched my husband's parents deteriorate mentally and physically and fade away, too. They were both cremated—their ashes scattered together underneath a tree in a forest near Gatlinburg, Tennessee.

I've lost pets, and I've mourned for them, too—sometimes

more than I've mourned for people who've passed away.

But back to my cousin's funeral.

Yancey's niece, Ashley, stood up in front of all of us and shared some lovely memories. I admired her courage and composure and wondered if I could push my pain aside for ten minutes and speak about a loved one at a funeral service. I'm not sure.

After my cousin's burial, I gathered my passengers and drove off into the blazing sunset while Mom, my stepfather, and my beloved Aunt Gloria recapped the events of the preceding days. They talked about how good this person looked and how bad that person looked. They talked about who brought food and how delicious so-and-so's cake was. They talked about relatives that didn't attend the funeral or burial service and speculated as to why they didn't show up. They talked about Yancey, and what a beautiful little boy he had been so many years ago. They talked about my Aunt Joyce and wondered aloud about her future. They talked about life, and they talked about death—sometimes in the same breath.

I've reached an age where my parents and my remaining aunts and uncles are all surpassing the average life expectancy. Friends and contemporaries are fighting and losing battles with cancer and other debilitating illnesses. I find myself thinking about mortality more and more these days. I brace—not for my own decline and death, but for the eminent loss of the lights around me who brighten my world.

My mother has always talked candidly about death, dying, and the afterlife. A few years ago, she called and told me matter-of-factly to prepare for a whole slew of deaths in our family.

"There's no easy way to say it, so I'm just going to come right out with it," she said. "We have so many in our family who are either really sick or really old, so be prepared. When they start dying, they'll drop like flies."

Mom suggested I keep at least two appropriate funeral dresses in my closet at all times and urged me to make sure my husband's suit still fit him, which I did. She also said, "You might want to plan and visit with some of your family that you haven't seen in a few years. You never know—you may not get another opportunity to spend time with them."

Her words made me sad, but her warning proved to be prophetic. Mom's always on the mark.

As far as her own death, Mom talks about that, too, even though she has the health and stamina of a woman half her age. For the last several years, she regularly sends me a spreadsheet that itemizes all of her bank accounts and personal business. She's given me a copy of her will and a key to her safe deposit box. I know exactly where she wants to be buried—beside my father's body at the cemetery east of Collins, Georgia.

Her main concern is my stepfather, Johnny.

"If I go first, please *be there* for him," she has pleaded with me. "He's going to need a lot of love and care. I know you will help him in every way that you can."

And I will.

Yes, I've seen death, and I understand both its finality and its truth. Like Forrest Gump's mother said, "Death is just a part of life." It reminds us of what's important—that we are only here for a finite number of days, that we should live each day as if it is our last, that we should love one another, that we should show compassion and forgiveness to others, and most of all, that we should never take one moment for granted.

Vickie McEntire

Calhoun Area Writers Treasurer

Vickie McEntire writes about things that are important to her—literacy, community, human profiles, and most of all, *family*. Her work has been published in *Chicken Soup for the Soul: Inspiration for Teachers, Telling Stories: a Calhoun Area Writers Anthology*, *Lady Literary Magazine, Dalton Living Magazine, Calhoun Magazine,* and on her blog at www.aliteratelife.blogspot.com.

She released her first children's book, *Baby Birds*, in October 2016. It was nominated for Georgia Author of the Year Award. She says she was inspired to write her children's book by her three grown children and grandson— her real life *Baby Birds*.

Empty Nest, a book of poetry illustrated by local artist, Sandy Dutton, was released in May 2017. Her second children's book, Little Bird and Myrtle Turtle, was released in October 2017 and is available on Amazon and at Barnes & Noble. It has also been nominated for Georgia Author of the Year Award. Vickie is working on several projects, including her debut novel, *Tucker*

Hollow, a Southern novel set in the summer of 1979.

She is an active supporter of literacy (Calhoun-Gordon Council for a Literate Community and the Ferst Foundation) and promotes reading—specifically reading aloud to children—by making appearances at local schools and libraries. She mentors the next generation of writers and attends writers conferences and workshops throughout the Southeast. She is a member of the Society of Children's Book Writers and Illustrators, Georgia Writers Association and Calhoun Area Writers group.

Aside from writing, McEntire also works full time and manages a photography business. She writes from her home in Northwest Georgia, which she shares with her husband, Dave, and their cat. Join her on Twitter (@vickie_mcentire) and Facebook (@BooksbyVickie).

A Broken Vessel
Vickie McEntire

Does not the potter have the right to make out of the same lump of clay some pottery for special purposes and some for common use? Romans 9:21 (NIV)

I received a stoneware creamer with no lid in one of those games we play at Christmas to exchange gifts. It had muted blue and white horizontal stripes. I recognized the brand, Pfaltzcraff, but thought to myself, "What an odd item to bring as a gift." Of course, I knew the brand from collectible Santas and cookie jars given to me by my previous mother-in-law.

I took the creamer home with a feeling it was a special piece, but for the life of me I couldn't figure how why. So it went to the top shelf in the kitchen cabinets, where other rarely used items lived.

I glanced longingly at the "vase" every time I opened that cabinet door to retrieve some other dish. I had come to think of it as a vase, because I didn't drink coffee and knew it would never be used in my home as a creamer.

One day I placed it on the counter and it got knocked off and broken. I was crushed in a way that defied explanation. I had never used this piece of pottery, but it was mine, and I thought it was beautiful regardless if it was useful. I carefully picked up each piece with no other intention than to put it back together. I never entertained the idea that the vase would no longer be useful. I just glued all the pieces back to where they fit. After that incident, I could not put the vase back in its hidden storage. Now it seemed even more special. As I moved my fingers around the set pieces, and felt the roughness and accepted the holes that now existed, I acknowledged that this vessel, in this condition, would not be able to perform as it was created to. It could not contain liquid. I could not let go, so I gave it a special place to wait for its purpose to come along.

A time came when we were collecting pennies for a program at the church for feeding the hungry. We were all provided with a small box to put our change in. The box would be kept at the table, so it would be a convenient reminder to us at each meal, and we would let our children bring their little colored boxes to the front of the sanctuary to pour our gifts into a larger container. I knew in that moment that my family would collect and transport our pennies in a very special vessel.

The broken vessel became the centerpiece at meal times. It proudly collected and held our gifts and on Sunday mornings, my children carefully carried it to the larger container and returned to the pew with a broken, empty vessel that returned full every week.

This would seem like the end of a cute story, but years later the broken vessel came to Sunday school with me when I was teaching the teenage class, and became a symbol of myself, or someone they knew, or even one of them. I told the story as they passed the vase around the room. Each one of them handled the broken vessel as if it were a precious piece of crystal. They understood the symbolism. I felt emptied that day, and knew that I, as a broken vessel myself, was of great value to the one who fills me up over and over again. I would not be able to do the job that some like me were created to do, but I could pour out gifts into the larger container, too. My gifts would be different than the gifts of others. Nonetheless, my gifts would be added to other's gifts to make a better world. My holes would not be removed, but I was whole and useful and still beautiful.

The Oostanaula River
Vickie McEntire

A drop of dew from the dawn of a new day fell on the sleeping soldier's face. He was too dehydrated to confuse it with sweat or tears, even though his daily efforts warranted the first, and the devastation he had witnessed, the latter. The volley from midnight still rang in his head like the morning after moonshine. He batted his eye lashes. The intruding sunlight entertained the previous days' images of fire blazing sideways and stopped only by the trunk of tree or man. He could hear the Oostanaula River as it surged southwesterly with its' secret. There were no signs of the turbulence caused by Sherman's crossing of the steep, muddy banks. Morning had been broken by flames and the dark smoke swirling from the burning bridge and railroad tracks set fire by Johnston.

The waking soldier's heart sank once his mind, fully awake, remembered the task that waited. The smoldering from two days of cannon fire caught in his throat as he muffled a cough with the back of his hand pressed against his parched lips. *There must be a canteen out there.* He added canteen to the list of things he would look for when he went to forage in the field. His back ached as he rose from the cool, moist leaf bed and peered through the tangled trees at the silent battle ground that held his day's labour. He knocked the leaves off his lower body, noticing yet another item he needed to acquire. *God, my feet are going to fall off! I should have no trouble finding a pair of shoes in my size.* He vigorously rubbed life back into his limbs, and ignored the growling from his abdomen. He looked to his right and to his left as groaning came from both sides. His comrades were still with him. They, too, struggled to face the impact of the previous thirty-six hours.

"Up and at 'em! Daylight's a burnin'!"

The groaning increased while the other men slowly moved to a semi-sitting position. They were hunched over. Their uniforms, dirty and ragged, no longer fit. Hollow eyes stared from angry faces. They looked more like a new species of animal, no longer civilized humans.

"We got a lot of work to do today. If you thought the last couple of days was hard, you ain't seen nothin' yet," the leader began his pep talk. "Keep your mind on the task at hand. Don't look in their eyes." He gave advice even though the others seemed not to hear. Their responses were barely audible utterances.

The men slowly tromped through the undergrowth that led to the open meadow. The sun warmed their backs. Even though they knew what to expect, the sight uncovered by morning light pulled a gasp from the group. As the men bent over each mutilated body, they were envious of their fellow fighters who were now marching onward in the direction of Adairsville. The first thing they checked was the shirt pocket. Every soldier carried with him a reason for fighting; that was in his soul, but a clue to his identity would be on his person. A photo of a loved one might be kept in the shirt pocket, close to the heart. A Union soldier would more likely be wearing a metal disc on a string around his neck, upon which would be stamped United States War 1861, the soldier's name, his unit and the name of his hometown. Many Confederate soldiers, not being able to afford an identification tag, and fearing their bodies would not be identified in the aftermath of battle, simply wrote their names on a piece of paper and pinned it to their clothes.

Every note or photograph collected represented another sacrifice made for the cause, but it also helped each side to keep a count of their losses. As they gathered the valuable and the priceless, the men on burial detail were grateful they didn't have the task of informing the widows of their new marital status. Eerie silence followed them from corpse to corpse as the midday sun beat their brows and vultures circled above. Countless faces were recognized. The men carefully wiped blood from the photos found too near the injury. They picked up "minnie" balls that had missed their mark, which was rare due to the spent bullets' long-range accuracy.

As night fell, the men left the grounds thickly covered with dead heroes and their indispensable mules and horses. The tired looters were drawn like moths around the campfire.

"Look what I found on a poor Reb," one of the soldiers half-grinned as he held up a flask.

"We can use it to wash down this corn pone I got from…" The soldier's voice trailed off, because they actually knew the unfortunate Confederate soul that had carried the homemade bread in his haversack.

The flask of whiskey provided by the unlucky demise of a Union soldier was passed around the circle from lip to parched throat as they tallied the loss of life for both sides. There was plenty of hard-tack to go around, because most of the fallen soldiers carried the hard, cracker-like biscuit with them. A chunk of salt pork was not offered, as that solder kept it hidden for consumption later. A handful of raw coffee beans roasted near the open fire, as a few hard candies that had been plundered were divided between them.

Tomorrow we will feast on horse, the leader thought. The soldiers were too tired today to even push a body into a shallow grave, much less pull a horse to their campfire.

Beside each of them was a pile of objects that would tell the story of the Battle of Resaca. The men had stopped counting at 5,000. One by one, they gave in to the soothing power of the whiskey to ease their pain. Dew drops kissed their heavy eyelids goodnight, and the Oostanaula River roared past the carnage without saying a word.

The Shirt off My Back
Vickie McEntire

Truly, I tell you, whatever you did for one of the least of these brothers and sisters of mine, you did for me. Matthew 25:40 KJV

The sporadic knocking interrupted my reading. I was home alone. I could smell the alcohol before I got the door fully opened. She frequently walked the neighborhood in this condition.

She flashed an intoxicated smile and said, "I need a favor, honey."

I pulled the door open wider. I had no idea how she thought a teenager could help her.

"I wanna go to church, but I don't have a dress."

I could help her. I listened to her explain why she drank. In her mind, a new dress was going to be the catalyst to the change she needed—and that change would be found in a pew on Sunday morning. I thought she wanted one of my mother's dresses, since they were closer in age, but she wanted to see mine. I opened the closet door and let her have her pick. She took two. I don't know if she ever went to church, but she no longer had the excuse of having nothing to wear.

I had heard the old adage many times growing up—*he'll give you the shirt off his back.* The phrase goes back to the 1700s and is fairly self-explanatory. To give someone the shirt off your back means you are sacrificing something; being extremely generous.

As a child, I understood it to describe a helpful person, even to the point of removing his own clothing. I had never witnessed anyone taking his or her shirt off and giving it to someone in need. As an adult, my understanding of the saying evolved to a person being *willing* to give something they owned to someone else who needed it more.

We were poor, but I watched my parents enact this expression of love over and over. We had families over for Sunday dinner after church, even though we bought our groceries with

Food Stamps. If someone needed a couch to crash on, ours was available. Car broke down? My dad was a skilled mechanic. Need an ear to bend? My mom was an expert listener.

We also learned by experience how to receive with humility and thanksgiving. *Privileged* was not in our vocabulary. Since I grew up on the receiving end of giving, giving became an unsurprising extension of receiving. It's funny how the universe recycles that way. When someone admires something I have, or says they need something, I hear it as an invitation. I've never really had extra income to make large charitable donations, but I have found myself frequently encountering individuals whom I could help.

One rainy afternoon, my sister and I were having dinner at Waffle House to celebrate my last day as a single woman. I had just slid into the booth, when the smiling waitress complimented my yellow slicker.

"I need one of those," she said.

"They have them at Walmart," I told her. "Ten or twelve dollars, I think."

She shook her head, and I immediately understood that look—no extra money. I had planned on doing a little pre-wedding shopping with my sister, so we headed to Walmart after we ate. Fifteen minutes later, that same waitress was smiling at me again as I handed her a brand new, yellow rain slicker. She looked like a couple of raindrops had landed in her eyes, even though she was still behind the counter working her shift.

It was a natural progression for me as an adult to volunteer at my church to deliver meals to the hungry once a week. My children rode along and even helped hand the plates to those confined to their homes. We were delivering more than just food— we smiled, said "Hello," and

asked how they were doing. My last stop was a sweet old lady who lived alone. I always packed extra plates, because she always invited us to join her for dinner.

The opportunity for generosity extends far beyond clothing. I've given away jewelry, books, money, food, toys, and kindness. You get the idea. I'm always open to the possibilities that may cross my path.

I visited my uncle in the hospital. He had just learned he had lung cancer. He was going to fight it. I stayed long enough to listen to him tell stories about his childhood. According to him, I didn't know what poor was. He grew up picking cotton and going to school with no shoes. He remembered one Christmas, when he was four or five, wishing for a red fire engine, but being disappointed when he got a bag of fruit and nuts.

I left the hospital with a mission. Even though it was July, I was able to procure a shiny, red fire engine. I caught a glimpse of that little boy from long ago, when my uncle opened the gift wrapped in Christmas paper. He laughed…and cried. The toy was displayed proudly on his mantle. He died in October of that year.

At my doctor's office, a teenage girl complimented my dressy jacket. Of course, I thanked her. Thinking back, I don't even remember what the jacket looked like, and it makes me chuckle to think I might have worn something someone half my age would find appealing. I slid my arms out and offered it to her.

"Here, try it on. See what you think."

She tried it on, and was still convinced that she liked it.

"Keep it," I said, smiling.

"Oh no, I can't do that," she argued, but I insisted.

When I visited my mother in the hospital just before she died of cancer, she said, "I like that shirt you're wearing. You look so pretty in it."

I said, "Thank you." It was one of my favorite shirts. She wouldn't have bought something like that for herself, but it sure did look pretty on her against the pink silk background of her casket.

If we think our possessions are worth something because we own them, we are missing their true value. Whether it is a dress, a rain slicker, a jacket, or a blouse, the blessing of charity begins the very moment we learn to recognize an opportunity to share with others, and act on it, wherever and whenever it is presented.

Walls

Vickie McEntire

The bottle of Gray Goose Vodka had cost $900. It was enclosed in a silver wire cage. The drink could be purchased without the enclosure for $160. The value was in the barrier.

Her neighbor said, "It's criminal not to let that caged bird sing." The neighbor, a fat, dirty, alcoholic old man, offered to buy it for $100. They laughed at his proposal, and it perched on display on the top shelf for years. Then, the neighbor's wife died. They gave him the prized liquid for Christmas. They warned him to be careful with the distilled beverage, because it could be dangerous.

Days later, smoke billowed from the neighbor's backyard. He had started a fire to burn a small pile of dead leaves. They went over to help him extinguish the fire, but it had grown out of control by the time they climbed over the wood fence. His passed-out body was stretched across the concrete steps of the patio. His right arm extended in an open handshake and the empty bottle at his fingertips.

"Daddy!"

Her scream disappeared into the same thin air as the spilled spirit.

***

"Something there is that doesn't love a wall…" she read from his favorite poem at the funeral, "…and makes gaps even two can pass abreast." The days preceding had been medicated, which allowed her to entertain memories she had long suppressed.

"You were exactly what he wanted—" she had been told frequently about her father's expectations for his firstborn, "a blue-eyed, bouncing, baby girl." That was the preface to many of the recollections her mother had shared with her when she was a young girl.

She remembered the two of them watching WWF (World Wrestling Federation) on the big screen in the living room. At every chance, one of them gave the other the "elbow drop" to the shoulder. A quick wince of pain from one was followed by a delayed belly-laugh from both. Saturdays were spent fishing and waiting for hours for supper to bite. Stories of the one that got away were told while eating the one that got caught. She waited patiently as he took old televisions apart just to see if he could reassemble all the parts correctly. They cheered in unison when the tube displayed a picture again. He put her behind the trembling handles of a garden tiller. She learned the parts of his 1965 Mustang—gasket, piston, camshaft, and spark plugs. Under his supervision, she took the engine apart…and put it back together. He gave her the car on her fifteenth birthday.

Soon after that, things were different. She was different. She became a woman.

Often, she had wondered if she had been born a boy, would their jovial relationship have continued unchanged into her adulthood. The invisible wall was not discussed, but its existence was very real. You couldn't do an elbow drop over it or get a fishing pole under it.

She hadn't tried to tear it down. It was comforting just to know he was on the other side.

"Walls are visible everywhere we look," she said. The audience in the chapel was small, but she hoped her words might have a ripple effect. "Much planning and intention go into their construction. They keep our neighbors on the other side. They shelter unwanted animals and care for orphans. They protect us from inmates and the mentally ill. The world cheered when a certain wall was torn down. Some people cheer now at the promise to build a great new wall. All of these physical walls represent something." Tissues raised to dab eyes around the room.

"Fear...and separation." She dabbed her own eyes.

"We are driven by fear to build walls to separate us from that which we fear. Walls allow behavior not tolerated in the light of day. They allow people to forget what they knew. Walls block the light. They prevent crossing from one place to the next. Daddy has climbed that final wall." She bowed her head and fought hard for the courage to finish.

She continued reading from the poem, "We keep the wall between us as we go."

Muffled crying could be heard from several bent heads.

"Before I built a wall, I'd ask to know what I was walling in or walling out."

Millicent Flake

Calhoun Area Writers Secretary

Millicent Flake is surrounded by books in her job as media specialist for Valley Point Middle School in Whitfield County and loves helping young people get excited about reading and writing. She has met many great writers through the Calhoun Area Writers, as well as the Georgia Romance Writers and Georgia Writers Association. She has written for *Calhoun Magazine*, *Dalton Living Magazine*, and *The Nerdy Bookclub Blog* and was published in *Run for God Devotionals 3*. She is currently working on her first novel. Visit her blog, *Under the Magnolia Tree,* at maflake.wordpress.com.

The Real Deal
Millicent Flake

Grace can be a tricky thing. Sometimes it slides in unnoticed and sometimes it comes up and slaps us in the face. Last summer it slapped me in the face.

I was spending several days in Atlanta with my dear friend Mera Corlett, "Susie" to me and our other friends from 35 years ago when we were students at Southern Baptist Seminary in Louisville. We met up for the Cooperative Baptist Convention and although the programs and services were inspiring, the best part for me was the time for heart to heart talks with Susie, one of my true soul sisters.

On Thursday one of our good friends, John Talley, drove in to have dinner with us. John has pastored Southern Baptist Churches for the last 30 years and is one of the most sincere guys I know. He picked us up at our hotel and took us to Mary Mac's Tearoom, an institution in Atlanta. I felt like I was back in my Grandmother's house in South Carolina. The restaurant is in an old building and features good Southern cooking - and lots of it!

We made the mistake of ordering the Southern special - 3 meats, 3 vegetables, homemade yeast rolls, cinnamon rolls, corn muffins and dessert. Just before the waiter brought out a huge platter of fried chicken, green beans, fried okra and squash casserole, John took out a small black bag and excused himself.

"I've been diabetic for 30 years," he said, "and I have to go give myself an insulin shot."

I was surprised to hear this, since he is the picture of health, but I admired his matter of fact attitude. When he returned we dug into the fantastic food and had a wonderful time laughing about old times and catching up on everyone's family news.

We did our best with the huge amount of food, but there was no way three normal sized people could eat all of it. Susie and I were heading back to the hotel, so we insisted John take home all the leftovers. The waiter brought two Styrofoam boxes and John filled them up and put them in two plastic bags.

The restaurant was ready to close as we finally pulled ourselves up from the table and stepped outside. Rain was coming down, so John, always the Southern gentleman, told us to wait and he would get the car. As Susie and I stood in the doorway of Mary Mac's, I watched John head down the street. A homeless man on a bicycle stopped him and they talked for a minute. With no hesitation whatever John handed over one of the bags of food, nodded to the man and went on his way to get the car.

Susie and I looked at each other and she had tears in her eyes. "He's the real deal," I said. We were so proud and happy to have that kind of friend, who after 35 years of preaching and teaching was still compassionate to the old black man. I know some people are cynical when it comes to homeless people, especially those that ask for food and money on the streets, but what I saw in John's action was the true heart of a Christian minister - one of God's children was hungry and without even thinking about it, John gave him food.

Susie and I were still waiting on John a few minutes later when the man on the bicycle rode up.

"Were you all with that man that gave me this food?" He asked. When we said yes, he continued. "I went over to get out of the rain to eat it and found this." He opened up the plastic bag and there was John's black insulin shot bag, sitting on top of the Styrofoam box.

This was when grace slapped me in the face. This man, who in the eyes of many is at the bottom of the social strata, had the dignity to come back to find John to return the insulin bag. He could have tossed it, or sold it to some crack friends, but he realized that the bag was important. Now yes, he did mention he could use some bus fare, and Susie quickly gave him a few dollars. Maybe he just brought it back because he thought he could get some money, but I don't think so. I think John had treated him with respect and he was responding to that.

On the surface it would seem that these two men have little in common - John is a successful minister with a loving family and a comfortable home. He has worked hard to be well educated and to make a good life for himself and his family. The homeless man, on the other hand, is probably not living an easy life, either through poor choices, addiction, mental illness or just bad luck. Yet both are the same in God's eyes, sinners in need of grace.

These verses from Romans have deeper meaning for me now:

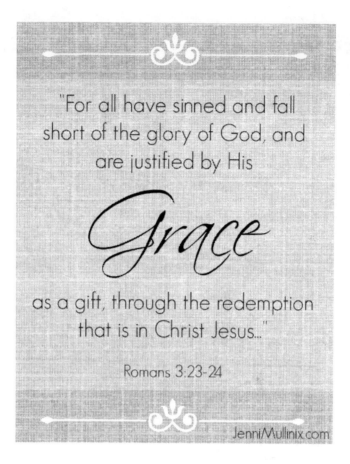

"For all have sinned and fall short of the glory of God, and are justified by His

Grace

as a gift, through the redemption that is in Christ Jesus..."

Romans 3:23-24

JenniMullinix.com

Brian Grogan

I was born of Truett and Peggy Grogan in the early summer of 1960 at 3 AM. This is probably the only reason that would keep them to keep them up all night until a Sunday morning.

We lived in many places where we would follow my Fathers profession, however finally settled in Smyrna GA. This is where I attended and graduated from Osborne High School. In February of 2004, I made the decision to move to a smaller town, and as I had friends in Calhoun GA and this is where I chose to live.

I am the author of the book entitled

Daily Applications of Unconditional Love (Using Spiritual Principles Effectively)

- o   You can find it on the web at
  https://www.createspace.com/5972360
- o   ISBN 10- 1523205756
- o   ISBN 13- 978-1523206759 (Create Space assigned)

God's Love
Brian Grogan

Love does not label a fish as stupid for not being able to climb a tree. Love is Kind; Love is Patent and does not insist upon its own way. God's love endures forever. This is based on a quote by Albert Einstein.

God is love and love is giving but God does not always give me what I want, or what I think I want. One day I was walking thru new places in life, that I was more afraid not to pass anymore, I began to find the answer to this question. The main thing God wants from me is that I don't hurt myself and many of the things I thought I wanted, in truth were things that would hurt me ether because I wasn't ready to use them without hurting myself in some way I did not understand.

A persons weakness isn't something to take advantage of or make fun of, but rather it's a opportunity and with some people rarer than others to express God's love' To let one self-love a little more effectively each day paves our path to happiness in life.

If exercise is easy then the results are minimal at best and soon one loses trust and thinks it is a waste of time for them. If one seeks only to have love and compassion for those they relate to, or feel comfortable with before they should have love and compassion given them; then are we really exercising our spiritual principles such as love, compassion and understanding? Alternatively, are we merely hypocritical of our own words while and accepting our own lack of growth?

No greater gift I know then the honor of being of service to any other God has to cross my path. Thank You God for the honor of being an earthen vessel of your love. Thank you for allowing us to give your love freely to whom so ever I find along life's journey.

The prayer of purest motive with love in their heart and the faith that God loves all as much as He loves any is the greatest force there is. For life within creation is merely an exercise to learn to love others more than possessions, titles and such things.

God make me an instrument or your peace and love of which no weapon forged by man can penetrate. Its strength is the ingredient that binds unconditional love with the compassion of God. God's love endures forever without end.

God bless the heart of man however best you know to help the seeds of love grow. That it be your will, not mine. and

May the light of God's love and compassion lay lightly and

yet distinctly upon and before You this day and may all that read and those effected by them be greatly blessed without end with love that endures forever

The greatest way to destroy those that would seek to be our enemy is the most power of force there is. With the prayer and actions to expressions of God's unconditional love to them, for from such a defense, man can forge no weapon and in time, those that identified there self as our enemy can become valued Friends as God's love endures

May those of broken heart today find comfort and motivation in the midst of their suffering let themselves move forward to let their selves love them self with God's unconditional as well as seeking to care for others during the search for the clearest path of life thy can find before them

God help me not to judge others as well as myself with earthly eyes. Instead, please help me to see us one, loved with your eyes. God that I might honestly speak love and compassion with my lips as well as thru the actions with my hands to who so ever I meet along life's path.

Kay Whatley

Kay Whatley is a teacher, gardener, and homemaker living in Northwest Georgia. She is the mother of four grown children and a grandmother of ten. She wrote and published a community newspaper, "The Shannon Spark", for ten years. At present, she is enjoying retirement with her grandchildren and keeping active with her gardening and teaching Sunday school.

Lilies
Kay Whatley

Lilies don't work
Lilies don't spin
God does it all for them.

Neither can we work
Neither can we spin
To make a life worthy of Him.

It's Jesus's righteousness
It's Jesus's atonement
That make us his.

Make our works His works
Make our deeds His deeds
Make us like Jesus.

Gene Magnicheri

Gene Magnicheri lives in Armuchee, Georgia with his wife Gina. While most of his writing experience comes from the technical writing done as an engineer, he greatly enjoys other forms of writing. Devotionals, short stories, and journaling have all become creative outlets that have produced materials he uses in his ministry. Gene has actively been involved in Men's Ministry for over 15 years and is currently leading a weekly study at West Rome Baptist Church.

The Letters of Peter

Gene Magnicheri

The following is a sample of a devotional series on First and Second Peter. The plan is to make this a 30-day devotional that will take the reader to an in-depth study of these letters.

Introduction to the Letters of Peter

1 Peter 1 (HCSB)

[1] Peter, an apostle of Jesus Christ: To the temporary residents dispersed in Pontus, Galatia, Cappadocia, Asia, and Bithynia, chosen [2] according to the foreknowledge of God the Father and set apart by the Spirit for obedience and for sprinkling with the blood of Jesus Christ. May grace and peace be multiplied to you.

2 Peter 1 (HCSB)

[1] Simeon Peter, a slave and an apostle of Jesus Christ: To those who have obtained a faith of equal privilege with ours through the righteousness of our God and Savior Jesus Christ. [2] May grace and peace be multiplied to you through the knowledge of God and of Jesus our Lord.

The two letters Peter wrote to the Churches in the Asian Minor are the only writings we have from the Apostle that remain with us today. It is for this reason, that the limited communication of this Apostle should be thoroughly studied and understood. To gain an understanding of message that Peter was communicating to the early church, this devotional series will look at the broader picture of the two letters. Stepping back to see the big picture will be helpful in getting a better understanding of the message that Peter had sent to these churches. While Peter was writing to a very specific group of people in the early church, his words still apply and are directed to all believers throughout the ages.

In examining the larger perspective of Peter's writings, the connection between the two letters becomes very evident. In the first letter, Peter gives believers an idea of what the Christian life looks like. He walks believers through the process of understanding the new life, which grows out of the new birth, born of God. He also lays out what a follower of Christ should expect in their day-to-day life and the attitude that should prevail in the life of a believer.

With the theme of the first letter in mind, the major point of the second letter is revealed. Peter opens this letter by pointing out that we find all we need for life and godliness in Jesus. In the first letter, Peter tells us what the Christian life looks like and then in the second letter he explains how it is applied to everyday life. The second letter seems to complete the thought of the first.

I would suggest reading these two letters together and prayerfully consider all that Peter is saying. I believe in doing so, you will have a clearer picture of what the Christian life looks like and find the sufficiency to live the life that God has created you to live.

The Aliens
Gene Magnicheri

1 Peter 1 (HCSB)

[1] Peter, an apostle of Jesus Christ: To the temporary residents dispersed in Pontus, Galatia, Cappadocia, Asia, and Bithynia, chosen [2] according to the foreknowledge of God the Father…

Keeping with the custom of the day, Peter clearly states who the letter is from and who it is addressed to. While the first few verses seem to be nothing more than the customary greetings, careful consideration and meditation does bring to light other information Peter wants to convey.

Peter first introduces himself as an apostle of Jesus Christ. He wants to make it clear who has sent him and the authority that comes with the message being sent. It is because Jesus has given the title and authority to Peter that Christians should listen to what the Apostle has to say.

The recipients of the letter are the churches of the Asian Minor, who Peter addresses as temporary residents. This description serves to remind the readers of their true earthly status and the circumstances that lead to their displacement. The reference to the dispersion seems to refer to a particular event, which modern scholars assume has to do with the persecution of Christians by the Romans. Peter is not clear about the event or situation he is referring to in his letter, but refers to common knowledge, which was known by the writer and the letter recipients. This missing information does not dull the message or take away from his meaning. What is to be understood is that the home of the believer will not be found in Rome or the Asian Minor, so do not get attached to any one place.

In these opening verses, Peter also stresses the providence of God, letting these people know that there was purpose and meaning behind their dispersion. Everything that happens passes through the hands of God first and does not happen by chance. Later in this chapter, Peter stresses how the Gospel message has spread because the imperishable seed of God, which is God's Word, has been scattered all across the land (see 1 Peter 1:23). While it is God who provides the imperishable seed, He chooses to let man be the sower that plants the seed in the heart of others. This is a very important principle Peter clearly points out. God delights working in and through man for His purposes.

Peter's reference to these believers being dispersed brings to mind seed that is scattered across the land to bring forth new life where it is sown. Each believer has within them the Word of God to share, so wherever a believer goes, the imperishable seed of God goes with him. The Master Gardener intentionally sent out believers in all areas of the Roman Empire for His purposes. Even through persecution by man was meant to destroy Christianity, God used it to make it flourish. Nothing can stand in the way of God's purposes, not even the Roman Empire.

The Elect

Gene Magnicheri

1 Peter 1 (HCSB)

...chosen [2] according to the foreknowledge of God the Father and set apart by the Spirit for obedience and for sprinkling with the blood of Jesus Christ.

In the opening verses of Peter's letter, it is quickly understood that there is nothing that can work against God's plan or purpose. The seeds of God's Word will be scattered where He wills and there is nothing man can do to prevent this. Therefore, it is obvious that God has a plan and is intentional in His thoughts and actions. It is also obvious God delights in working in and through man to establish His plans and purposes on earth.

To emphasize the sovereignty of God even more, Peter tells the churches that God chose them long ago. Before time began, God had laid out His divine purpose to bring salvation for sinners to fulfillment in the life, death and resurrection of Jesus Christ. It is by God's great plan He had predetermined the way to have an intimate, saving relationship with the elect.

What makes the plan a reality is the sanctifying work of the Holy Spirit. Faith, repentance, regeneration, and adoption are all the sanctifying work of the Holy Spirit in an individual. It is the work of the Holy Spirit that sets a person apart for God's purposes and separates him from the world. The sanctification process is an ongoing work which continually makes a believer more and more like Jesus.

For what purpose has God chosen us and for what reason has the Holy Spirit sanctified us? All for God's plan, to obey Jesus. It is our purpose to become like Christ, "being created in Him for good works, which God prepared beforehand so that we would walk in them" (Ephesians 2:10). We were created to be conformed to Christ and to obey Him. This is what it means to be saved. Thus, when a person comes to faith in Jesus, they are making a pledge to obey Him. Peter points out this responsibility of every follower and then seals this pledge by sprinkling the blood of the Sacrifice on the people. In verse 2, Peter is referring to an act that Moses did at Mount Sinai (Exodus 24:8). Moses had read the book of the covenant to all the people of Israel and the people responded with a promise to obey all that was in the book. To seal this deal, Moses took the blood of a sacrifice and sprinkled it on the people. This act at Mount Sinai was a shadow of what was to come. It is by the blood of Jesus, the true Sacrifice, that our pledge has been sealed and fulfilled. Our obedience does not come by the will power of man, but is guaranteed by the resurrection power of Jesus to give new life and by the sanctifying work of the Holy Spirit to live it out. As Peter will point out in the opening of his second letter, we have all we need to live the life we are called to live. It has all has been accomplished by Jesus.

Be Ready To Use Words
Gene Magnicheri

1 Peter 3:14 (NKJV)
"...always be ready to give a defense to everyone who asks you a reason for the hope that is in you..."

Are you ready to give an answer for the hope you have? Can you do this in a way that makes sense to someone else? It can be very hard and a little intimidating to express the transformation in your life and the hope you have. This is something that goes to the depth of your being and is not easy to share. To open yourself up and reveal this very personal and private part of yourself is to make yourself vulnerable. It is natural to want to avoid those situations where you are uncomfortable and vulnerable, but Peter is asking you to be ready to do this.

Many Christians will often say that their life is a testimony to the world and words are not necessary. Believers are called to live a life of holiness and it is true that this call is a part of our witness to the world. In fact, the major theme of Peter's first letter has to do with how Christian are to live. Peter tells believers they are to live their life in such a way that the world will come to glorify God because of their good deeds (see 1 Peter 2:12). Yet this still falls short of being a full expression of the Gospel message. While people will be able to see the character of Jesus in you, they will not come to know the message of the Cross or the hope you have because of Jesus. When Peter tells believers to be ready to give a reason, he is telling them that sooner or later, you will have to use words.

It is by God's Word that you were born again and it is by spreading the seeds of the Gospel others will be born again (see 1 Peter 1:23). Knowing this, Peter gives the instructions for believers to be ready. People will see your life and know you are different. They will see your hope is not in this world or the things of the world. They will see the love of Christ in the way you serve a broken and fallen world. You will shine like the lights of a city on a hill for all to see. Your life will have an impact by preparing people to ask questions. What will be needed then is the power of God's Word to speak new life into a person. It is truly amazing and a privilege that a sovereign and powerful God entrust us to share this message. God uses us as the great means to bring transformation to a person's life.

In the next devotional, Peter tells us his choice for the greatest evangelist, which is the one he wants the church to follow, Noah. The reason for this choice may surprise you.

The Greatest Evangelist
Gene Magnicheri

1 Peter 3:19, 20 (NLT)

"[19] So he went and preached to the spirits in prison— [20] those who disobeyed God long ago when God waited patiently while Noah was building his boat. Only eight people were saved from drowning in that terrible flood."

The previous devotional talked about Peter's instruction for all believers to be ready to use words to spread the seeds of the Gospel message to the world. The main point Peter is making in this part of his letter is the importance of believers to be ready and able to express the hope that is within them (1Peter 3:13-22). It is by this very personal and intimate way of sharing new life that God has chosen to expand His Kingdom. In doing so, God's providence and power is magnified even more because he uses the weak to do the impossible work of the strong. God could demonstrate His power and might by working out His plan by Himself. He is God, He can do whatever He pleases. However, God has entrusted man with His Word to go out into the world and share this wonderful message. Only a sovereign, powerful God could do such a work to accomplish His perfect will.

Peter then presents to us his example of a great evangelist who spoke the Gospel Message, Noah. I have to admit, this would not have been my choice of a great evangelist. Why would Peter choose someone who lived thousands of years before Jesus to be a great witness? Looking at Noah's success as an evangelist is not impressive either. There were only 7 other people who got on the ark with Noah and they were all family members. He had 120 years for his words to have a transforming effect on people and yet there were no other salvations. By man's standards, we would call his ministry a failure. Yet, Peter says that Noah is a great example and one for the church to model.

Peter uses Noah as the evangelistic model of the church for one main reason. It was because of the judgment of God was at hand. There are only two times when the judgment of God falls on all of mankind. The first was in Noah's day and the other will be the final judgment, when Jesus returns. Noah was called to declare God's truth prior to the flood. The church has the same call. We are to declare God's truth until Jesus returns.

Another reason Peter choses Noah is because of his faith and obedience. Noah believed God and did all that God commanded. Noah preached God's message just as he was told. Salvation was not Noah's to give, it was God's. God gave the opportunity, but as Peter points out in his second letter, this was the most resistant people who had ever lived (2 Peter 2:5). So, in reality, Noah's ministry was successful. The success was not because of the number of people saved but because of his faith and obedience. Remembering this principle takes all the pressure off you and places the responsibility where it belongs, with God. All you need to do is to be faithful to your calling.

Janette Stephenson

Dear Readers,

I've always been a curious, analytical, talkative type.

For example, I never use to hang up on telemarketers. After they gave their pitch, I'd query them about their product or services and ask all the impossible questions I could think of to learn how they handled objections. Then I'd spend some time sharing with them on how to perfect their pitch and responses so they could get a positive outcome.

Don't get me wrong, I didn't buy anything from them and I usually told them to remove me from their call list (unless it's a robo-call with a recorded voice on the other end – then I just hang up). But I don't hate telemarketers the way some do.

I've had many a friend ask, 'Why do you bother? Why don't you just hang up? Why are you wasting your time explaining to them how they should do their job?' But the way I figure it, since it's their job – and one I think must be a really hard – they have to be good at it to succeed. I've even had a few telemarketers thank me for taking the time to help them. I consider it a learning opportunity; a kind of pay-it-forward – because I've been lucky enough to have people take time to share their wisdom with me, which ultimately helped me through life.

And that goes for my writing. I have no problem speaking stories. But to put them on paper is quite another feat. If it were not for generous people taking the time to help me understand the creative writing process, I would have never been able to put pen to paper in a meaningful way.

My background is in the hospital and healthcare industry. My career in business primarily consisted of working the front lines to initiate constructive dialogue and critical thinking processes regarding mergers and acquisitions between healthcare companies. My analytical brain helped me greatly in this endeavor. And though I've always had a deep desire to write creatively, my left brain inhibited my ability to engage my creative side. But with the guidance of some great people, including members of this club – Calhoun Area Writers, I have evolved and made progress with my writing. I started a novel, *The Buttercup Premise*, and I've included two of its chapters in this Anthology. I hope you enjoy them.

Whether you are looking for an engaging read, or encouragement with your writing, I hope you'll take the time to read our 2018

Anthology. And remember to 'share your wisdom with others', perhaps even with someone who may not realize – until much later – how you've helped them. Your wisdom is a gift.

Wishing you only the best,

Janette

The Buttercup Premise
Janette Stephenson

Spending the majority of my childhood playing outside in wide open spaces, under blue skies, and within dense mountain forests, did more to free my imagination than any teaching offered by formal schooling.

My Mom and Dad gave up their business careers when they adopted my brother and me. They decided, rather than raising us in a big metropolitan area, to buy a farm and introduce us to country living. Both of them had been brought up similarly, so they had a mutual appreciation for the fact that in the country you breathe fresh air, see stars at night, actually hear the rain when it falls on your roof, and the birds who sing when the rain stops. They believed learning how to rely on yourself and each other, and tending to chores – gardens, animals, and such – would provide a hands-on learning experience that would serve us well during life. They were not wrong.

To start a typical day, Momma would make a huge breakfast which I'd scarf down in ten minutes flat, and that included going back for seconds. Then the screen door would slam behind me as I ran to get Celeste from the barn.

She'd always hear me swing open the oversized wooden door. And I'd usually find her standing on the edge of the hay loft peering over the side and meowing down at me; which I always pretended was her '*good morning*'.

Celeste was an unconventional Siamese cat. Her striking blue eyes and brown and silver features looked stunning in the coats and capes I occasionally styled her in, which were really make-believe clothes I made using scraps of old cloth I'd found around the barn. We often played dress-up on rainy days. But on sunny days, an outside adventure always called. And Celeste tagged along.

My friend Angie never believed my cat walked with me wherever I went. She said only dogs walk with people, cats just sit and watch. I wanted her to meet Celeste and take a walk with us. We even hatched a plan to walk towards each other's house, meet in the middle, and then walk back to my house. But it never happened. Though we were neighbors, Daddy said four miles was too far for little girls to walk a dirt road all by themselves. He said we'd have to wait until we were at least twelve before he'd allow that. Daddy was a hardworking man who barely had time to eat and was too busy to cart us back and forth just for fun-time. Even as a child I realized this, so I never played the '*but please Daddy*' card.

Some days Celeste and I would trail through the edge of the forest playing hide and seek. She always found me before I could find her. Occasionally I'd saddle up our white footed quarter horse, Ginger, for a ride through the fields. I typically took Celeste along in a pack I'd carry on my back, leaving the top open so she could enjoy the view too. Both she and Ginger tolerated each other effortlessly unless there was a jump involved. If Ginger and I decided to get rowdy and leap a few fences, I'd put Celeste down on a perch of some sort. Then we'd swing by and pick her up before heading on down a path.

Other days, Celeste and I would play in the creek that ran across the edge of our property. She always watched from the creek bank of course. I, however, had no problem wading knee high in rushing water, feeling the mossy creek bottom between my toes, while trying to catch her some lunch. Sometimes I was lucky enough to catch a tadpole. But those darn little fishes always escaped my small hands. Still, I'd pretend to bring her a feast when I climbed out of the water. She was polite and stood regal as I laid my catch before her. But she never did more than sniff at my offering, or occasionally play with it if it happened to move.

No matter what we did on sunny days, there was one thing that was a ritual: we'd walk to our secret hiding place in the middle of the six acre pasture behind the barn. That's the field where Ginger and our other two horses lived. Sometimes the cows and goats would wander through, but they rarely stopped. Instead, they'd usually head for the blackberry bushes or the tall grass on the far side of the field to munch all afternoon.

That pasture was an amazing and magical place. Especially because right in the middle, for about one square acre, there grew nothing but mounds and mounds of buttercups. It was a sea of huge yellow flowers for Celeste and me to play in. The buttercups grew so thick and tall that when I laid down among them, I was nowhere to be seen. I disappeared. So when I got tired or just needed to think things out, I got horizontal and watched the clouds float by. And without hesitation, Celeste would crawl up and sit on my stomach. We could stay hidden for hours.

Sometimes I'd hear Daddy yell out to me from the fence behind the barn. He'd call me back for dinner or occasionally as a warning about a storm headed our way. But I never gave up my hiding place; especially since Daddy told me not to linger in this part of the field. I never really understood why because he and Momma liked the flowers I put in our vase on the dining table. But when he called out for me, I'd peek up and wait to see him walk away before grabbing Celeste to take off running. He'd usually be pitching hay or doing something to the tractor by the time I got back to the barn. He always knew I'd come when called though.

One day I waited for Daddy to turn away, but jumped up too soon. He had turned back around because one of the horses in the field behind me had whinnied back at him. I squatted back down. He called to me again. I didn't answer or stand up, but knew better than to let him call again. So once he turned back towards the barn, I stood up with Celeste in my arms and slowly started my walk across the pasture.

When I reached the barn, Daddy was inside feeding hay to our cows. He stopped and turned towards me, "Young lady, why are you hiding in that field of buttercups? You know I told you not to go into that part of the field."

"But Daddy, I pick buttercups for our flower vase all the

time," I said in a whining tone. "They're my favorite flower and there are tons of them in the field. We don't hurt them. We play in them."

"Honey," he said tenderly, "I know they're pretty to look at. And it's okay for you to put a few in a vase to enjoy. But I told you – you have to be careful because buttercups can be poisonous."

"I don't eat them Daddy."

"Do you think you have to *eat* buttercups for them to steal your life?" he asked as he wiped sweat from his forehead, then took a knee to get eye level with me. "Look… do you remember Mr. Wolf?"

"Yeah," I said grinning, "but he likes to be called Chief Wolf. I like that big feather headdress he wears sometimes."

"Well, Chief Wolf told me an Indian story about how buttercups use *trickery* to poison people. He said after the bulbs sprout up through the ground, they create a poison powder that covers their flowery buds. But they make themselves so beautiful and grow in such gigantic bunches that no one can resist picking their yellow blossoms by the handful. Unfortunately, when people stand in their fields and pick their bouquets, the petals gradually release their poison onto the hands and feet of the picker, which eventually blisters their skin and devours their soul. Chief Wolf's people even believe picking a single bloom can foretell the misfortune of how this poisonous flower preys. That's because the picker, unaware of the consequences, holds the bloom in their hand until the flower wilts, which is pretty fast, but still too long."

"So the flowers are really trying to poison me?" I asked.

"Actually Kimberly, the way I see it, the flowers are trying to get '*you to poison yourself*' by touching them for too long," he suggested.

"How many buttercups do you think it takes to steal a soul, Daddy?"

"I don't know honey, but any poison can cause trouble," he stressed.

"But Celeste and I love to lay in the field and watch the sky. I've even fallen asleep there," I confessed.

"I've seen our herds avoid those yellow blooms and I'm surprised Celeste goes near them. Does she lay on them too?" he probed.

"No," I admit, "she just walks around unless I lay down, then she lays on my stomach."

"See, she knows not to lay on the flowers. And you should stay off them too," he warned again.

"And you really think they can steal my soul?" I ask.

"Well that's the premise. So no more laying in the buttercup field or I'll take the bush hog to them, okay?"

"But Daddy, they must like me because I haven't been poisoned," I pout.

"Like Chief Wolf said honey, it's rare for someone to survive the poison of the buttercup," he reached out and tousled my ponytail, "and I don't want anything to happen to my sweet Kimberly. So from now on, you can *only pick a few* – and you have to put them in the vase in the house *right away*, okay?"

"Okay," I agreed.

With that, he got up, turned and went back to pitching hay.

Celeste and I started strolling towards the house. As we walked along I looked over at my feline friend and asked, "I wonder how many buttercups it would take to poison me?" Celeste meowed back but I didn't bother to interpret her response. I was too busy thinking about how many beautiful soul snatching flowers it must take to steal my soul because I've been around them almost every day since I was old enough to wander the farm on my own.

I began thinking I should probably start keeping count though. *But how should I count? Should each time I visit the deadly field count? Or, should each time I pick these flowers count? The next time I see Chief Wolf I will ask him how to keep count.*

In the meantime, I decided since I had not been affected so far, I'd count each visit to the field separately. And so it would be. Each time I came close to soul snatching trouble it was *"One Buttercup," "Two Buttercup," "Three Buttercup,"*...

"Am I weaving or something?" I rant towards the back window to the motorist behind me blasting their horn. I glance at the white lines on the road for assurance. This Jerry-Springer-like-day I just experienced was impairing my ability to focus on this curvy Peachtree-Something road traffic.

"*How* could he have been married to three women at the same time?" I protest to Angie, slapping my palm against the steering wheel. "Three! How can someone pull that off for two years without anyone suspecting anything?"

Angie looks at me with a baffled glare, "Kimberly honey, I honestly don't have a clue. That whole thing was so wild!"

Approaching the red light, I shift down into first gear. "Left or right?" I ask, pulling into the right lane and pointing up to the street sign, "Peachtree NE, or Peachtree Boulevard?" I shake my head in annoyance and add, "Hey, aren't we already on Peachtree?"

Angie grabs a folder from the passenger door pocket, "Kimberly, I know you've been out of state for a number of years, so let me just ask; did you forget Atlanta's known for their over two dozen Peachtree-Something roads?"

"I didn't forget. I just don't remember it being this confusing."

"Well hang on… let me find our hotel address." Angie puffs on her cigarette and riffles through the folder full of confirmations, tickets, maps, and documents we'd stashed for reference.

She grips one of the printouts and begins to study it; while I watch gray smoke swirl across the dashboard. My attention drifts back to the day's earlier events. All the disturbing stories my newly found birth mother had confessed… like how I had almost died in a fire three months before my second birthday.

A fire had begun in the middle of night, spreading rapidly through the women's shelter where she, among four other mothers and nine children, had found temporary housing. As soon as someone smelled smoke and yelled 'fire', screaming women started grabbing children and heading for the door. All the mothers, including my own, somehow failed to notice a crying baby standing in a crib. They managed to yank out eight kids from the blazing and smoke filled building. But when they got outside and started counting heads, mine wasn't one of them.

My mother claims she ran back towards the house to get me but two firemen had held her back. She recalled yelling out that I was still in a room at the top of the stairs. One fireman took off running, jumping the porch steps two at a time, into what was, by then, a kindling firebox. Less than a minute later he came running back down the steps, coughing and choking, but with me in his arms. My mother said he'd gotten there just as the wall behind the crib became swallowed by flames. She explained how he'd really been my hero that night.

When I asked how the fire got started, she stated they were later told it was 'of unknown origin', but most of the women suspected it was somehow related to the landlord. He'd recently inherited the shelter and made no beef about wanting to sell the place. And as soon as he collected the insurance money, a for-sale sign went up in the front yard. Though I don't remember that particular incident, I did remember the one she described that happened two months later.

Mother divulged that, at 15 months old, I was found lying, near-death, inside a cardboard box in an old abandoned house. I almost threw up hearing the story and kind of fell into a fog as she told it, making the story to seemingly unfold in slow motion. Not because it was so out of the ordinary from all the ghastly stories she was in no way bashful to share, but because this specific tale brought clarity to a nightmarish memory I'd had for as long as I could remember. I awoke many a night in a cold sweat with an unexplainable sense of desperation. Until today, I never knew what was causing such an intuitive response.

I asked her how I was found, but she didn't know. Said some state worker had come around asking questions. She told them that after the fire she had placed each of her children with a different extended family member because none of them could take all three of us. Not one was a person of abundant means, so we got shifted around a couple times. It was never determined who was supposed to have been caring for me when I disappeared.

I, of course, found that hard to believe. *Buttercup Two*, I thought, the fire had to be *Buttercup One*.

But her storytelling led to how my sister, my brother, and I ultimately ended up in an orphanage six months later. It was actually sad. On the surface, my rational mind was telling me it was just the result of bad luck and bad choices, made by poor and way-too-young kids having kids. I learned my mother was only sixteen when she had me, and I was the youngest of three. Hearing these facts quickly unclouded my mind. But as soon as I came out of one shock, I kind of fell into another, during a kicker of a story about what led my birth parents to break up in the first place.

That was a story I simply couldn't wrap my mind around – learning what my birth father, Edward, had done. That tall, strapping, gentle sounding, seemingly sensible man had been such an intolerable rat to my birth mother. Living three separate lives, three marriages. How their divorce eventually resulted in them both leaving the state, remarrying, and beginning all over again with different spouses. I learned I had nine half brothers and sisters from those separate families.

Mother and Father went on to share stories about how each of their new family members had faired throughout the years. They were proud of some and embarrassed by others. Both said they'd stayed in touch with Doreen, my older birth sister. And both said they often thought of me and my brother. And yet I heard no evidence either had tried to connect with us. I simply can't fathom how I'd come from such an absurd group of people.

Pulling me back from my thoughts I heard Angie rattling on, "I can't tell from these directions; they seem all backwards now. We're gonna have to call the hotel to figure out how to get back. I got my cell. Where's something to write down a number with? Better go left here," she points her index finger across the dashboard, "and then get on the Interstate about a half-mile on down, 'cos at least I know we need to head south."

"Sure. But I'm in the *wrong* lane." I grumble back to Angie, then pause. "But hey," I continue, "I just found out – that's the story of my life!" With this comment, my eye catches Angie's and we explode into laughter.

When the light turns green, I try to compose myself, turn on the blinker and check the rearview to see if it is safe to merge.

Angie's cackling turns to snorting by the time I eventually inch the car over to the left lane.

When I finally get the chance to pull onto the fifth Peachtree-Something I'd been on that evening, my side ached from laughing and my eyes well up from comical tears. Wiping droplets from my eyes and cheeks with my forehand so I can see to drive, I step on the gas and we head toward Interstate 295.

"My God, I can't believe that's my gene pool," I mumble and look over at Angie. "Can you believe those are *my* people?"

"Well honey," Angie says, trying to keep a straight face, almost holding her breath in the attempt, "I wouldn't exactly call 'em *your* people. I mean after meet'n your mother and sister yesterday, then meet'n your father with them today, my guess is nobody's more of a black sheep to a family than you are to yours!"

Angie was trying to encourage me, but I know we're both simply too stunned for either of us to absorb anything like that right now. I can only shake my head as I work my way through traffic.

"Are you going to call and get directions, or what?" I remind her, as she continues to fight laughter, enthralled in the details of accompanying me to my second meet-the-birth-folks event.

Angie throws her cigarette out the window. "I'm sorry. I'll call now," she says, her words interwoven with snickering, "let me get my phone." Angie clears her throat, grabs a pen from the glovebox, digs through her purse and pulls out her cell and dials.

While Angie calls the hotel for directions, I take the ramp onto the Interstate and head south. I feel some relief as I merge through thick lanes of cars and trucks into the 70-mile-an-hour lane. It seems comforting somehow for the car to be moving faster than my thoughts.

"We gotta go 'bout three miles," Angie says, closing her cell. "It'll be on the right. Just off Exit 44… also known as 'Peachtree *Avenue*'." She starts giggling again.

"Hey, you know what?" Angie asked. "When your father was telling us about his being married to all those women, I remembered Thanksgiving two years ago when you had Aaron over for breakfast, Lance over for lunch, and Doug over for dinner – without any of them seeing each other."

I shoot her a confused gaze, "Wait a minute. Are you saying I *am* like my father?"

Angie tries to stop laughing but can't contain her smile and a snort, "No. No, I don't mean that. I only mean him having to cope with all those women at the same time reminded me of that Thanksgiving."

"But I wasn't married to those guys!" I snap in defense, then add in a matter-of-fact tone, "And none of them had a family to be with that day. I was just being hospitable."

"I know. And I don't mean anything in a bad way. I just mean to juggle that many people at once takes a skill most people don't have. I don't know how you did it. I don't know how he did it. But I do know it takes some major organizational skills! Maybe you take after your father just in that one way."

I don't answer, my eyes remain fixed on the road as my thoughts try to keep pace with the surrounding cars. Finally, words explode from my mouth, "My God, three marriages at once! I couldn't have done that. Besides, it's wrong. No wonder things fell apart so badly."

Angie tosses the pen and folder back in the door pocket and stuffs her phone in her purse, "Hey, I don't know 'bout you, but when we get back to the hotel, I think we need to grab a drink. What d'ya say?"

I hear her, but am too busy thinking to answer with more than a quick, "Okay." Angie's comment has me speculating about other similarities that might exist between the man who feels like a stranger, but whose life resembles mine in at least one regard.

I was only with them for roughly two hours and had left completely stunned. How many more stories like these can there be? Thoughts swirl around in my head as my eyes fix on taillights down the highway. *Boy, Dr. Lee is going to love hearing about this.* I'm curious if he, being a therapist, is used to hearing such real-life nonsense. Suddenly, I had another thought; *I bet he'll like hearing about 'why' my birth sister wasn't there during my initial phone call to this wacky clan. Because she was in jail!*

I look up and see the large green 'Exit 44' sign. I'm ready for that drink Angie suggested. I glance over at her, "Hey, looks like this is it." I put on my blinker and slow down, "When we get to the bar remind me to tell you *why* Doreen was in the slammer when we first got into town. I forgot to tell you and, trust me, you are not going to believe it."

"No way! I can't wait to hear about that," she gasps and continues, "I also want to know how you plan to explain all this birth family stuff to your Mom and Dad back home. And *please* tell me what you think will happen tomorrow at your wacky clan's family reunion?"

I pull into our hotel's parking lot and quickly shoot answers to Angie, "You're gonna flip; I don't plan to; and oh-my-God-I-can't-even-fathom!" I click the seatbelt off; open the door, step out of the car, and head for the bar.

Mike Ragland

Mike Ragland was born and raised in Lindale, GA where he attended and graduated from Pepperell Schools.

After graduating from Pepperell High in 1963, he joined the Navy and was assigned to the submarine , *The USS Chopper* (SS-342) and served from '63 to '67. During that time he served in the north Atlantic, Mediterranean, South America and throughout the east coast and Gulf of Mexico.

When Mike rejoined civilian life, he worked briefly laying carpet and was fired the day he planned to resign to join the Rome Police Department, where he served 40 years and retired as a Major. As a member of the force, he served as a motorcycle officer, patrol Sergeant, Shift Commander, and Captain in Charge of Detective Bureau. He also served as Juvenile Officer, as a liaison officer to Juvenile Court and Training Officer until 1999 when he was promoted to Major. As Major, he rotated serving the three major bureaus of the Police Department: Operations, Administration and Support Services. During that time he was also the principal grant writer for the Police Department, bringing in many Federal and State grants to secure police officer jobs, positions, and equipment, including the *"Call to Duty Monument"* that stands in front of the Rome Police Department today. He now serves as Councilman for the City of Cave Spring.

Mike was married to Martha Highfield on August 23, 1968, and they have one daughter, Bekki Ragland Fox, and two grandchildren, Caleb and Mattie Parris. He is an avid Crimson Tide and NASCAR fan. A much loved speaker and writer in Northwest Georgia. Mike is devoted to writing full times since his retirement from the Police Department in April of 2007. He and his wife currently live in Cave Spring, GA along with three aggravating cats and three dachshunds.

His previous books are: *"Bertha"*, *"Legend of the Courage Wolf"*, and *"A Time to Gather Stones"* and current book, *"Living with Lucy"*.

Mike can be reached at mikeragland6@gmail.com.

Cave Spring's Texas Ranger
Mike Ragland

After some twenty years the City of Cave Spring is getting its cemetery committee back together. We have a couple of beautiful old cemeteries in need of a little tender loving care.

We're fortunate to have Stan Rogers, Rome's cemetery director, and the Georgia Cemetery Association advise us on what needs to be done.

Being an amateur historian with a large interest in the Civil War, I was wondering how many old CSA vets may be at rest in our cemetery. Pat Millican at the library in Rome says she thinks there are forty-one.

I know W.O. Connor and Felix Corput of the Cherokee Artillery are there, along with some other community leaders. As I was scanning through them when I saw this 44 year old Georgia Militia Sergeant named Green Cunningham. I loved the name right away. I collect names I like for future characters in stories or books. How could you not like Green Cunningham.

In reading through his biography, or what there was of it, I saw mention of his Texas service. What Texas service, I thought. He was a Militia Sergeant. He probably fought in the battles around Atlanta, if that.

I make a call to Ann Montgomery and Pete Mathis. Do you know where this Green Cunningham is buried, I asked. An hour later I'm looking at his marker.

It says he was born in 1817 and left this earth in 1885. He was the son of James Cunningham I find out, who migrated to Cave Spring around 1830 with his brother Joe from Jackson County Georgia. It seems like they were friends of the Vann's and followed them into the valley.

Brother Joe soon moved on to Alabama and settled in Talledega, near where the speedway is today.

Henry Cunningham, one of Joe's sons recruited some local boys to head to Texas. It was 1834. The daughters of the Alamo verify that Henry and one of his brothers were at San Jacinto with Sam Houston. There is another Cuningham there also that has yet to be identified. It may be Green. We're not sure at this time, but I have a sneaking feeling it is.

He is listed on the muster rolls of Captain Caldwell's company of Rangers in 1839 fighting Comanche. And in 1839, the Comanche still owned about a third of Texas and they would kill you. Fighting them was not for sport, or the faint of heart. He is also mentioned in a couple of Journals, along with a William or "Bill" Cunningham.

In December of 1839 he was awarded 320 acres along the San

Marcos River near Gonzalez, Texas for his service. In his will, he leaves a two third interest in 502 acres of Texas land to his sister in Mississippi.

Yes sir, Ole Green Cunningham was a Texas Ranger. Wait a minute Mike. Maybe there was another Cuningham named Green. I thought about that. Here's what I was sent from Texas. In the May 14, 1874 Waco examiner there is a small article about a bunch of Baptist excursionist's from back east gathering in Waco. That's where Baylor University is located, still a strong Baptist school.

The article said many were first time visitors to the state. But it also says that others are returning after a long absence. It says Mr. Green Cunningham of Floyd County Georgia, one of the heroes of Texas Independence is back after twenty two years. That's good enough for me.

What is it about the Texas Rangers that makes the American public think so highly of them? They rival, if not exceed, the F.B.I. in popularity. I mean, good grief, John Wayne was a Texas Ranger in "The Comancheros," and there were Rangers in "The Searcher's," and "True Grit."

"The Lone Ranger" was a radio program, then a black and white TV show. Clayton Moore toured the nation having his picture took with every kid in the country. Clint Eastwood is a Ranger in "A Perfect World" with Kevin Costner, and there are

Rangers in "The Outlaw Josey Wales."

Lone Wolf McQuade, starring Chuck Norris, was the toughest Ranger ever. He followed that with the series, Walker, Texas Ranger. Have you noticed how the tough guys play Rangers.

I can't name them all. But I counted over 75 movies where the Rangers were featured or at least were in the film. During the "B" western heyday, there were 58 movies just in the World War II era that had Texas Rangers in them.

Who can forget retired Ranger Captains Augustus "Gus" McRae, and Woodrow F. Call played by Robert Duvall and Tommy Lee Jones in "Lonesome Dove?" What a great miniseries?

There is still a lot of work to be done on the Cunningham family, as there is in all of our cemetery residents. Many folks in Cave Spring have tons of information about their relatives buried here. Soon there will be some new software being created that will be second to none, and we hope we can accumulate as much information as possible about our cemeteries.

Best guess right now is that Green, who came back to Cave Spring and got extremely wealthy, owned a big farm where highway 411 and Cunningham road is now. I was told it was where the old wind wood swimming pool would be built in later years.

Green married Jincy Ware. She was a few years older than he was and died a few years before he did. They had no children, but funded and sent many a young person away to school from the Vann's Valley and Cave Spring area.

Green was a trustee at the "Cherokee Female Academy," later to become Shorter College. He stressed education strongly in his later years, and worked tirelessly to provide it.

For all you native Texans living in Rome and Floyd County, you have an old Ranger watching from the highest point of the Cave Spring Cemetery. He's still on sentinel duty. No, he isn't looking for Santa Anna's troops, or the Comanche.

I think he's there to make sure we abide by the law of the land, and hopes we obey the scriptures, assist in education, and to help those less fortunate than we are.

His stone is in need of a good cleaning, which it's going to get. It could use a foot stone for his Texas and CSA service, which it's also going to get. When you can, drop by for a visit. It's kind of peaceful.

Standing there looking at his marker, with the wind blowing from the west, I can hear the words of Captain Woodrow Call as he says "I won't tolerate rude behavior."

I don't think Green Cunningham would either.

Once upon a Waffle House
Mike Ragland

Last week it was early morning and I was on my way to finish up a few chores in Rome. First stop was Tractor Supply, one of my favorite stores anywhere. So, I thought I would stop at the 'Waffle House' and get me a chicken egg and a piece of dead hog, on the way.

I stop there a lot for several reasons. Mainly the food is good, the folks that work there are friendly, fast at their work, professional, and seem to be genuine down home folks. When I walked in, some waitress yelled 'come on in, grab you a seat and I'll be right with you.' I feel comfortable there.

I walk around the bar stools (too fat to sit there) and grab a chair at the short counter, kind of out of the way. Coffee and water appear as if by magic, order taken and I'm left to observe. There are several waitresses, and they're letting the Sugars, Baby, Darlings, and Sweetie's roll to all their customers, and accepting same from them. I chuckled and thought these country girls aren't afraid of "Sexual Harassment," they've heard it all. I imagine they think all of that we see in Hollywood and Washington is silly. Anyway, I like them and their attitude.

I sat watching the Big Guy doing the cooking. To be a short order cook, you got to get your act together. Watching a good one at work is a show itself. While waiting I let myself drift, all the way back to 1968.

We had just rotated to third shift. Boy was I ever tired of working a walking beat downtown. Third shift had its draw backs, but I was ready for the challenge. This was my first shift on third other than just a few days before Christmas in 1967. I was paired up with Archie Duvall (R.I.P. Archie) who was several years senior to me, and had worked third many times before.

I learned quickly there was nowhere to eat after midnight except the Krystal on Broad, and even it closed on Sunday nights.

Archie introduced me to 'Valley Vend' where they made sandwiches all night for vending machines they owned in the mills and companies around the county. They didn't mind if a hungry policeman came in and made themselves a sandwich. We ate a lot of Salami and pimento loaf, but they also closed on certain nights.

Josh Smuckler loved for us to stop in his store and also build a sandwich, and he had good Kosher meat, but he also closed after midnight. The same thing occurred at Roy's Little Garden (Roy's was open all night) on the other end of Dean Street. We appreciated it a lot, but you couldn't sit down and take a break with your meal, only at Krystal. At that time the one in West Rome was closing at night, and East Rome wasn't built yet.

Then one night we were told they were going to build a Waffle

House on Turner McCall across from the Methodist church. We watched it come up out of the ground for weeks. Then one morning there was a guy walking around inside.

We came to the door, but it was locked. He opened it and told us it would be a couple hours before his waitresses got there and started serving, but he had made a pot of coffee and we were welcome to have one with him, which we did and became the first two customers of a now defunct Waffle House.

In later nights I would watch him sling the groceries. He was good. The new restaurant was packed, which caused its own problems. After the bars closed, or the Black Clubs it was so crowded they had to make folks stand outside until one or two left, and then let one or two inside. The parking lot ran over onto the service station next door, and they complained. Parking on side streets caused residents to complain, and they complained about noise. Across McCall the eighteen wheelers would park, leave the trucks running, and residents on that side complained about fumes.

Aww, and then there were the fights. I guess the glass companies in Rome did a good business replacing the big windows or doors. Every Tusk Hogg in Floyd and surrounding counties was arrested there at one time or another for fighting. They were drunk, and fought over anything.

Even on slow nights we couldn't eat there. It always had a drunk or two that wanted to be your buddy. Hey, officer do you know old Bill Kinney, or Doug Williams. Maybe Bill Bohannon, or anybody on the department. You tell them yeah, and they'd name another. I mean they meant well, but it wasn't what you wanted to talk to a drunk about. Yes, there were drunken females too, and that's all I'm going to say about that.

I snapped out of my day dreaming as my order arrived. I get traditional Waffle House fare. I took my granddaughter with me before Christmas, figuring she'd never been. Ha, she ordered a triple hash browns with cheese, onions, jalapeño's, and tomato's. I'd never seen such a mess, and she ate it too.

Some of those waitresses now are prior military. It's a wonderful place. Looking around I didn't see any bullet holes, or blood spatter. The cooks don't have jailhouse tattoo's, and the waitresses are hardworking southern girls. Heck, they could pass for cowgirls too.

Before Christmas I gave each a copy of 'Living with Lucy' for their babies.

If you're close by when I post I'm there, stop and have a cup with me. May the Waffle House reign forever, just wish we had one in Cave Spring.

Cheryll Snow

God Bless!
C Snow
2018

Cheryll is an internationally published author. Her goal as an inspirational fiction writer isn't to preach but demonstrate the themes of love, family, faith, and redemption via real-life characters that today's Christian woman can relate to. She's also a wife, mother, grandmother, and Registered Nurse. Along with writing, she enjoys reading, gardening, travel, puzzles, and any project that stretches her creative muscles.

Her work has appeared in numerous publications, including Louise DuMont's Cup of Comfort blog; Cecil Murphey's Shattering the Silence blog; Amber Lanier Nagle's Project Keepsake; The Upper Room (pending); Chicken Soup for the Soul: The Dog Did WHAT?; Chicken Soup for the Soul: The Power of Forgiveness; Chicken Soup for the Soul: Inspiration for Nurses; Chicken Soup for the Soul: My Very Good, Very Bad Cat (Feb 2016); and The Chattanooga Writers' Guild 2015 Anthology. She is a frequent contributor to Lady Literary Magazine and won third prize in the Chattanooga Writer's Guild Annual Writing Contest, Non-fiction category. She is currently seeking representation for her first novel,

"Sea Horses."

She loves hearing from readers! Visit her website at www.cheryllsnow.com.

Missing

Cheryll Snow

Beatrice sits on the edge of the bed, her upper body tilted forward, like a baby bird leaning precariously out of its nest. Strange hands lift her arms and help her into her slip. She stares at the ebony face in front of her. She can't place the young woman as the aide applies a touch of rouge to Beatrice's cheeks and brushes out her silver-white hair.

Who let this person into my home?

She looks around. She doesn't recognize the room or the furniture. Through the doorway, she spies a china cabinet filled with dinnerware.

Those dishes aren't mine! Where is my crystal? My Hummel figurines?

A sense of panic begins to envelop her. *I can't stay here. I must get out!* Her hands smack the tops of her thighs, over and over. "Out!" she cries. "I want out! Out! Out!"

The aide takes hold of Beatrice's hands and places them in her lap. "It's okay, Mrs. B," she says softly.

But Beatrice doesn't believe her. She begins her chanting again in earnest. The woman draws her attention to the large picture window. "Look outside, Mrs. B! It snowed last night. Look how pretty it is!"

"Out! Ou..." Beatrice looks. The low sky is the color of steel and the trees in the distance are bare. Beneath the windowsill, a layer of snow covers the tops of the rhododendron bushes.

Like frosting on a cake.

"Pretty, pretty," she murmurs, staring out the window.

"You're right about that, Mrs. B," the aide tells her. She lays a skirt and blouse on the bed and Beatrice's attention is drawn to the faded quilt. She pushes the items aside and runs her hand over the fabric squares.

I know this.

Suddenly, she sees this same quilt stretched across the lower limbs of a magnolia tree. From beneath the canopy comes the sound of muffled giggling as Beatrice plays a game of hide-and-seek with her granddaughters.

"Now where can they be?" she asks in mock bewilderment. Peering into the open space, she sees the girls' small forms huddled together on the ground with their backs to her.

"Boo!" she calls out. The girls scream in unison, then burst into peals of laughter as the youngest falls forward, pulling the tent down with her.

Her reverie is cut short by the sound of the aide's voice. "Don't you look pretty today, Mrs. B?"

Beatrice smiles, not in response to what the aide told her, but at the laughter of her granddaughters echoing back to her through the crippled maze of her mind.

"Where are my girls?" she asks.

"Which girls you talking about, Mrs. B?"

Her train of thought is derailed, and she turns away.

The aide helps her into her stockings and shoes. Beatrice catches her reflection in the mirror. She doesn't recognize the image as her own. Gone forever is the pleasing figure that attracted many a suitor as she walked past. The youthful hipbones which cradled the weight of three unborn children have become porous and brittle with age. And her long, shapely legs, once considered to be her best asset, are now blue-veined and frail, as pale as the underside of a fish's belly.

The aide prattles on as she buttons Beatrice's blouse and skirt. Something about today being a very special day. But the words bounce off like pebbles against glass.

Shuffling down a short hallway, Beatrice stops in front of a grainy, black-and-white photograph of a young man dressed in uniform.

Phillip! That's my Phillip!

Her late husband's name reverberates in her head, first a whisper, then louder and louder. She smiles. She's fifty years younger, waiting at a train station.

Where was that?

She sees Phillip as he steps off the train, tall and handsome in his Army uniform, his duffel bag slung over his shoulder. A whistle blows. The conductor takes out a watch from his vest pocket and gives the final boarding call.

Chicago! That's where it was!

Phillip had greeted her that day with a chaste kiss on her cheek. He took her dancing that evening. And that was the night they fell in love.

Beatrice starts to hum a lyrical tune as the aide guides her through the entrance door to her suite. She can't recall all the words, but she remembers the last few lines as she and Phillip float across the floor.

"...Waiting 'round the bend... My Huckleberry friend..."

"What are you singing, Mrs. B?"

Beatrice's memories scatter.

She makes her way down a wide carpeted hallway to a large dining room. She sits at a large cherry table decorated with pine boughs and red candles. The sounds of music and muffled voices filter softly around the room. But it's only when a man she's never seen before, dressed in a charcoal gray suit, leans over to kiss her cheek and wish her a merry Christmas that she realizes the significance of the day. A woman in a red dress stands next to him, smiling. And for a moment, a spark is ignited in Beatrice's memory.

A tiny bundle wrapped in a pink blanket...

A smiling, dark-haired girl with one front tooth missing, holding tight to a tire swing...

The rustle of white taffeta and lace...

Just a flash…

Margaret Anne?

And then it's gone.

Dinner is served, and Beatrice looks down at the chain of holly leaves along the edge of her plate.

Like a necklace.

"Pretty, pretty," she says.

The woman in the red dress sits next to her. She talks quietly to Beatrice throughout the meal. Something in the sound of her voice makes Beatrice feel good inside. She's not sure why.

The ham tastes delicious. So does the cranberry sauce. Fresh, just like she used to make. But she doesn't touch her mashed potatoes.

No lumps. Must be instant.

Someone sets a slice of pumpkin pie in front of her. She stares at it. Something is missing. Then a dollop of whipped cream is placed on top of the pie and she smiles. She picks up her fork and takes a generous bite. The woman in the red dress laughs. Beatrice looks up to see everyone at the table smiling at her.

Back in her suite, the woman in the red dress sits across from her. She catches snippets of the conversation floating around her.

She nods off.

Beatrice awakens with a start. The woman is now beside her on the sofa, holding her hand in her lap and smiling at her.

"Mom, we're leaving now," she tells her.

That familiar sense of panic fills her, climbing upward into her throat. "Wh—who are you?" she stammers. "What are you doing here?"

She tears her hand away from the woman's grip. "Get out!" she yells. "I don't know who you are! Get out, I said!"

The woman in the red dress tries to comfort her. "It's okay, Mom. It's me, Margaret Anne. Don't you recognize me?" She reaches out to take Beatrice's hand, but she snatches it away and pulls herself up from the sofa.

"Don't you touch me! I don't know who you people are! You shouldn't be here!" She backs away toward the kitchen. She grabs a silver letter opener on the counter and holds it out in front of her. "Police!" she yells. "Help! Police! Somebody help me!"

A blur of white uniforms appear. Strong hands grab hold of her and pin her arms to her sides.

"Please! Don't let her hurt herself!" the woman in the red dress cries.

"Easy now, Mrs. B," a male voice tells her. "You're okay." The orderly pries the letter opener from her hand. Beatrice screams over and over again for someone to help her.

Another person enters the room with a syringe and Beatrice feels a stinging sensation in her upper arm. "What are you doing to me?" she cries. "Who are you? You shouldn't be here!"

Soothing voices reassure her as she is led back to the sofa and made to sit down. Within a few minutes, her mind begins to calm and her eyelids grow heavy. She's asleep when the woman in the red dress leaves with the man in the gray suit, her hand clamped over her mouth to hold back the sobs.

Strange hands again. Different face. Helping her put on her nightgown.

"Busy day, Mrs. B?" the girl asks.

She slides into bed beneath the cool, crisp sheets. The aide bids her goodnight.

Darkness.

Outside, it starts to snow again. Beatrice watches the fat, lazy flakes swirling around in the gusty air. Around and around… until they fall to the earth, silent. Like the ones captured inside those plastic snow globes she used to have when she was a girl.

The tune she was singing earlier in the day returns to her in the cocooned silence of her room. Her eyes grow heavy once again. Her last thought before falling asleep is of Phillip.

And in her dreams, they dance.

Marla Aycock

My debut into an author's world was in July 2014. My love of reading, journaling, writing song lyrics, letters, and designing greeting cards created a natural path to writing my daughter's memoir, *Grief Is Not My Future*—a raw and personal story of her journey through cancer. Writing has helped me process and heal while honoring the beautiful life she lived. My goal is to bring hope to all who struggle with the why's of suffering.

One of the best decisions I've made as a budding author was to join the Calhoun Area Writers. A group of literary talented people with a heart to support newbies like myself and cheer on all who share the passion of crafting words on the page.

With three years of membership in CAW, I've had the joy of working with CAW's talented leaders as we planned and executed the successful Northwest Georgia Writers Conference in May 2017. The crowning touch to light my literary fire has been the CAW Critique Group. I can't emphasize enough the value of belonging to one. The support, accountability, and encouragement provided from them are key to my staying the course.

I have had the delight to write three pieces published in CAW's 2017 anthology, titled "Telling Stories." I hope you will enjoy my true stories in our new 2018 anthology: "Feathers for Christmas", "Arrested", and "A Major Shift, Sealed with a Kiss".

I've spent most of my life in music education and ministry while raising a family of three daughters in Marietta, Georgia with my husband Keith. I presently live in Kennesaw, Georgia atop Brushy Mountain, a former Civil War Battlefield.

Spare time often finds me in my kitchen where I delight in creating homemade meals for my family, passing down my love of music to the next generation to my gifted grandson at the piano, and loving on my grandchildren brings laugh-out-loud-moments I'll cherish forever.

Other activities include hiking Kennesaw Mountain, exploring trails in North Georgia, swimming, and attending Women's Bible Studies. Oh yes, and lots of reading.

I'd love to hear about your own writing journey or what you think about our new 2018 anthology. Check out https://goodgriefgal.wordpress.com for progress on *Grief Is Not My Future.*

A Major Shift—Sealed with a Kiss
Marla Aycock

My life changed forever on a sultry August day in 1970.

Exhausted, I sprawled across the bed in our new home. My adventurous husband, Keith, who I'd dubbed as my Oklahoma Cowboy, bounced into the room with shocking news.

"We're moving to Atlanta!"

I said, *"Whhaatt?"*

Our fledgling family had just moved from Michigan, to the beautiful Pennsylvania Dutch country-side two months earlier for Keith's new job. Six months pregnant with an energetic one-year-old daughter—another move was *not* on my radar. Mild bouts of morning sickness still clung like unwanted clouds after weeks of rain. I was barely settled into the rhythm of our new life. I thought, *are you kidding me?* This had to be a bad joke.

So, why would I even consider this wild upheaval of a move? Me, mild-mannered Marla, and my Crazy Cowboy Keith, were polar opposites but attracted to each other like magnets. We were a Winnie the Pooh meets Tigger duo. I'd lived a well-ordered quiet life in one home with one set of parents. Keith's chaotic family moved a *lot* and his parents divorced when he was nine. Yet his faith, funny unpredictable antics and out-of-the-box thinking fascinated me. Wherever he was, I wanted to be.

The first year we were married, Keith opened an atlas of the United States and asked, "If you could move anyplace, where would it be?" I'd quickly placed my finger on Atlanta. Ever since my boss at General Motors visited Atlanta and raved about its beauty and charm, I'd wanted to visit.

Keith did *not* lose his job in Pennsylvania. A new business opportunity had opened up.
Mr. Biggs, a prominent businessman in Savannah had met Keith the previous year. Keith had shared his vision of starting a budget motel chain. During the short time we were in Pennsylvania, Mr. Biggs contacted Keith again and expressed willingness to invest in his dream.

Keith's first project—to explore the Atlanta area for potential building sites, was a perfect fit. I'd often told him, "You would have made a great scout master of a wagon train headed to the Wild West." Quick to assess situations, Keith loved being on the leading edge of whatever he was involved in.

Saturday, a week later, we loaded our U-Haul rental truck. Keith headed out first to fill the truck with gas and get on the road. We knew he'd be lumbering along at a top speed of 55 mph because of the speed governor on the truck. I'd easily catch up in my Pontiac GTO.

After completing some last-minute preparations, I set my one-year-old, Kristi, in the front seat beside me. There were no infant car seats or seat belts. Horrors, right? What must a Millennial be thinking right now? My little Kristi, would be a loose ping pong ball in a tin can zooming down Interstate I-81.

A drop of moisture slinked quietly down my neck, and a

summer breeze whisked through my damp hair as I drove off. I anticipated great adventures in this romantic historic city of *Gone With the Wind* fame, and I couldn't wait to explore it.

Heavy traffic filled all three lanes as we left Harrisburg, Pennsylvania. Kristi held her teddy bear tight as she climbed into the back seat and fell asleep. I'd traveled about thirty miles when young guys in a car to my right started waving and honking. I knew I appeared to be alone and thought they were flirting or admired my GTO. I accelerated, pulled ahead and ignored them. Before long, people to my left were waving. I'd heard people in the south were friendlier, but I wasn't even out of Pennsylvania.

Someone behind me laid on their horn long and loud. Alarm spiraled as I realized, *there's something wrong with my car.* Then I remembered straddling the loose scrap metal on the road. I slowed and eased right toward an exit ramp when I heard the muffled cry of a passerby— "…gas pouring out of your car!" A thought flashed, *one spark and we'd become an **exploding** tin can.*

I cautiously rolled into the one lone gas station. I explained my predicament to the attendant who said, "Well honey, we close in fifteen minutes and there's not much we can do until Monday. We're closed tomorrow, being a Sunday and all." My heart plummeted as I realized I had no way to let Keith know where I was. *I* didn't even know where I was. Cell phones wouldn't exist for another twenty-five years.

The jarring realization Keith had all our money and our one credit card brought a new dimension of panic.

Another man walked out of the garage wiping his hands on a greasy rag. He perused the back of my car and casually remarked, "I sure like your bumper sticker." I watched his countenance shift and soften as I remembered the words, "Wise men still seek Him."

He said, "I tell you what—I'll put your car up on the rack, empty the rest of the gas, and seal the hole with some liquid solder. I can't guarantee it will hold, but it may get you down the road and find your husband." I was grateful, but humbled, as I told him Keith had all our money. I offered him my pathetic three dollars but he wouldn't take it. Time passed and daylight ebbed. The solder seemed to hold and my Good Samaritan filled my car with gas. I thanked him profusely but left feeling so vulnerable.

I silently reasoned Keith would come back looking for me, but chances of finding each other along this winding wooded expressway was unlikely. Vision of oncoming cars was often blocked.

Failure to make motel reservations or set up a place to meet, was a costly oversight. Inwardly I ranted as a few hormonal pregnant tears leaked. All I knew to do was keep heading south. I navigated curves and scrutinized each oncoming vehicle when possible as emotions peaked and exhaustion threatened.

Daylight faded to dusk and then—there—lights flashed at me from the oncoming traffic. A U-Haul had never looked *so* beautiful. I pulled over as relief and fatigue collided. My scout became my hero.

We spent the night at a small motel in Northern Virginia.

The next morning an incredible sight met me. Large Luna Moths were resting on our door, windows, and lawn of the motel. A host of lovely, light-green angels. I stared in awe.

My mother, a naturalist, taught all five of us children to identify and appreciate the wonders in our world. We made more than one butterfly and moth collection. I'd longed to see a live Luna Moth someday. *This* was that day. They only live one week after hatching, so I knew this was a special moment.

After the turbulent start to our trip, I felt a seal of blessing on our new venture accompanied by dozens of light-green fluttery kisses.

We made it to Atlanta and our lives *were* changed forever. We'd found our true
North in the South—and forty-seven years later we still call it home.

Arrested

Marla Aycock

Haloes of dark brown hair encircle the cherub faces of Esther and Joanna as they were introduced as babies—the beginning of a life-long friendship. Esther was nine months and Joanna a mere three days old. It was the windy month of March and a timely gift of matching bonnets was the segue into the many inquiries as they grew. "Aww, are they twins?"

Our families were in business together so many days were spent in each other's homes. Joanna was the outgoing sanguine; a free spirit with energy oozing out of every pore. Esther was the quieter sensible one but with plenty of spunk and an eye for adventure. Together they created an interesting combination of fun, common sense, and mischief.

They grew up going to the same church, singing in musicals and Christmas pageants together. They took mission trips to the other side of the world and celebrated birthdays and major holidays in tandem.

While in high school, their youth group went on a ski trip to West Virginia. After a long day of skiing they pulled into their hotel parking lot still pumped from all their vigorous activity. Joanna, always on the lookout for boredom diversions, noticed the parking lot was shared with the West Virginia Police Department.

Not bothering to check in with the youth staff or chaperones at the hotel, Joanna and Esther headed across the parking lot seeking a new escapade.

Two apple-cheeked mischievous girls walked into the station and Joanna boldly requested a tour of the facilities. Heads snapped to attention as a wave of interest and shock registered on the officers' faces. Who would come into a small-town police station and ask for a tour? Maybe a grade school teacher or a local childcare director, but here were two adorable teen girls making this odd request. This was not exactly a big city precinct, so with amused smiles, the officers agreed and quickly embraced this welcomed diversion.

Delighted with their success, Esther and Joanna proceeded to walk through the offices, *ooohing* and *aaahing* over the jail cell, the officers' desks, and then the booking rooms. The officers drew the line when they requested to take pictures.

These feisty girls were just getting started with their antics as Esther announced, "This is our first visit to your fine state. How about some souvenirs?" Again, an expression of puzzled surprise spread across their faces. Good naturedly, one officer started digging through the drawers of his desk. He found some West Virginia State Patches, some stickers and other miscellaneous junk.

"Well, that's a good start," Joanna purred, but we had something more in mind, something cool—like tickets—real authentic West Virginia State citations. By this time the officers were getting into the fun of this witty caper. An officer looked at Esther and wrote her a citation for jaywalking. You could see the officer's eyes light up with mischief of his own when he looked at Joanna with a comical grin. He pointed as his words pounced and hit the target: "And *you*—Speed Talking!"

The girls noticed it was dark outside and knew they were probably being missed, but they were having too much fun to care.

In a pretty-please little-girl voice, Joanna asked the officers, "Would you grant us just *one* more favor? Would you call the hotel, ask for our chaperones, and tell them we've been arrested?" Totally caught up in Esther and Joanna's prankish-fun by now, their faces lit up like they'd just won the lottery. They were all in.

They made the call, cuffed the girls and packed them into the back of their squad car. A short time later the police pulled up in front of the hotel with sirens blaring and lights flashing. The chaperones and youth group members stood with gaping mouths and wide-eyed expressions as the girls stepped out of the back of the police car and were un-cuffed.

With arms wide and fingers splayed, together they said... "Just kidding!"

Feathers for Christmas

Marla Aycock

I felt suspended, left dangling in a foreign land. My movements mimicked a nomad trudging through quicksand. My voice was raspy from tears; I was trying to breathe but choking on life. How do you go through the motions of Christmas when death has swept through your world?

An indifferent mass of humanity swirled around me as I walked through the familiar doors of the supermarket. Habit carried me through the routine of buying a few necessary items. I made my way through the checkout line wrapped in my alternate universe. As I walked away the clerk chimed loud, "Happy Holidays!"

How strange, I thought, *why would she say that?*

The fog tilted slightly from my sluggish brain and I realized, *That's right, it is December.*

How can a person forget Christmas?

We had fought a six-year battle as we witnessed our precious thirty-two-year-old daughter, Esti, struggle against overwhelming odds to beat cancer. However, cancer proved to be the easy part of the drama which had played out in our family the last fifteen months of her life. But, there is no *easy* part of cancer. You know that, if you or a loved one has walked this valley. The cancer was hard, but the conflict among family members was another story.

Esti's marriage to a contentious controlling man had been in a downward spiral since her first cancer episode four years earlier. Angry at her choice of treatment and our support of her wishes, her husband shamed and bullied her as he spread fabricated stories and malicious innuendoes about our family. It created an atmosphere of suspicion causing loss of friends, reputation and the support we desperately needed. This web of lies eventually blocked our family's access to her when she died.

Emotionally drained, I found it difficult to function through the daily rhythms of life. Christmas gifts and normal holiday celebrations were lost in a background of hazy gray lethargy.

Happy Holidays?!

Resentment rose and the clerk's greeting echoed and clanged as I loaded groceries into my car.

Back home, spirit sagging, I mechanically placed grocery bags on the counter and headed to my room—crumpling on my bed like a used paper sack. Rest escaped me and before long I slumped to the floor in front of my dresser. A cushion of carpet softened the moment as I sat deciding whether to open the drawer. Some personal items of Esti's, were tucked away inside—remnants of her five months stay while convalescing in our home.

Tear-scorched eyes, sore and irritated from months of sorrow, caused me to hesitate as the salty droplets swelled and spilled once again. My throat felt swollen—as the usual lump formed—yet I needed the physical connection beyond abstract memories.

As the familiar items came into view, I reached for her jacquard black and white scarf, buried my face in its soft fibers and inhaled the scent of her. Sliding my fingers tenderly across her journals I knew I would always cherish these artistic well-told stories.

Then, I smiled large as I uncovered her Audrey Hepburn sunglasses. How she loved this star from the golden age of motion pictures. Images of Audrey graced the walls of Esti's bedroom during her teen years and eventually her guest room after her marriage. My grin broadened as I remembered our special chick nights snuggling on the couch, watching every movie from *Breakfast at Tiffany's* to *My Fair Lady*.

As I shifted her belongings, I discovered several miscellaneous gifts she'd overbought online the previous Christmas. The gifts never reached who they were intended for. As I gingerly embraced each one I suddenly knew I was looking at this year's Christmas gifts.

I thought, *These, yes these, will be **my** gifts to our family this Christmas!*

Like seeds sprouting into new life, I'd wrap each one with a note worded as if from Esti. I knew who each gift was meant for. We were kindred-spirits. I knew her heart. Her essence through these gifts would soften the blow of her absence and help fill the empty space left behind. It would give a meaningful path for my grief, and a way for our family to mourn together while honoring her memory.

A beautiful Christmas miracle began to unfold which defied the sadness, and uncovered a path through the heartache. Warm tentacles of life began to flow through my grief-clogged veins.

Sliding my laptop from the nightstand, I went to work. Two jewel-feathered headbands lay before me. Gifts I knew would go to Esti's dearly loved nieces, Tia and Cassidy. At a loss for words and looking for inspiration, I googled the word *feathers*. The Native American significance of these symbols popped up on my screen. Startled, my stomach did a wild flip as I thought, *What are the chances? Tia and Cassidy are part American-Indian!*

Feathers in the Native American culture symbolized trust, strength, power, and freedom. The gift of a Bald Eagle feather was a great honor as they believe eagles are a noble bird and have a special connection with heaven.

The words flowed from my fingertips, pouring life onto the page—words which reflected the love Esti had for these dear nieces:

Wear this gift and remember me.
You came from a long line of strong noble women.
Be trustworthy and walk in the power and freedom
God sent to you that first Christmas through His Son.

I riffled through Esti's collection to find the next gift. As I removed her journal a bookmark fluttered to the floor in front of me. Stunned, time seemed to stop as my eyes scanned the familiar Psalm.

*He will cover you with his **feathers** and under his wings you will find refuge;*
His faithfulness will be your shield and rampart.
Psalm 91: 4 NIV

Sometimes the thin space between the natural and spiritual amazes me. Esti, a graphic designer, had created a bookmark of this beautiful Psalm when her cancer returned. Along the side she had designed a feather disintegrating, but transforming into birds taking flight. She'd kept it close to her throughout her cancer journey and read it frequently. How prophetic.

Our Esti-Bird had taken flight, but in her absence, this first Christmas she'd left feathers to remind the next generation of God's faithfulness.

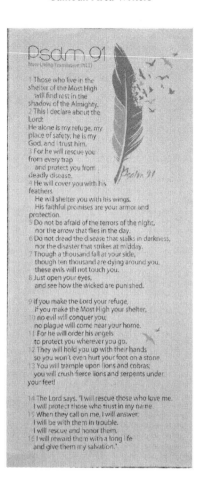

Gordon Flowers

Gordon was born to James L. and Margaret K. Flowers in New Orleans, Louisiana on April 12 1967. Due to James's job at the Milwaukee Railroad, Gordon lived in several locations before settling in Rome, Georgia. After school, Gordon did some traveling himself while delving into the Radio, DJ and Acting businesses, living in places such as New York, Colorado and Michigan. He came back to live in Atlanta Georgia and began living a wild out of control life style. While writing a dark satirical and blasphemous script mocking the Christian faith, he eventually found Jesus Christ, changing his entire life. He eventually settled down and moved back to Rome, GA where he follows Christ to this day.

Me & Jamboree
Gordon Flowers

Hello, my name is Darwin...last year I decided to become a big brother! I enrolled in a local big brother/ big sister program and expressed my interest in giving someone smaller and less fortunate than I was, a person that they could look up to. I had a older brother growing up and figured I could share everything I learned from him. They thought that was just swell!

Anyway, I asked if they and had any red or yellow kids lying around, or better yet any black or brown ones, you know...like the movie stars always get...but all they had was a white one! Ugh! Everybody knows white kids trend low on social media but I kept my trap shut like a grown up and took the little vanilla fella home.

So, what's your name, I ask. Trevor, he says. Trevor?! Trevor sounds like a kid who'd start crying if his ice cream didn't get any sprinkles on it! No way! Your name's Jamboree!

Anyhow, I brought Jamboree back to my trailer around noon and figured it must be around his feeding time. I was making him a peanut butter and jelly sandwich when I suddenly realized I didn't have any milk! "You gotta have milk with peanut butter Darwin, them's the rules," as my big brother used to say to me.

I told him to stay there and guard the place because the parks had a lot of break in's recently, while I run out and grab him some.

Well...he says he can't because he's lactose intolerant. Can you believe that? I informed him that "we were liberals" and liberals don't do intolerance. You follow?.. But I digress.

When I get home with the milk, I notice the little racist flipping through my very expensive comic book collection! That bigoted brat got his sticky little fat peanut buttery fingers all over my number one issue of the marvel spotlight series featuring Moonknight. I beat the crap out of him and told him to stay outta my room!

Well, the 'baby' starts crying. I felt kinda bad because he's only 11, so I figured I'd share a beer with him. His first! Memories, right? Then I had another great idea! We'll watch a movie together! I found out he'd never seen the Exorcist before..seriously! So I invited a couple of my drinkin' buddies over to make a day of it! Before long though, he starts screaming about nightmares! It's just a movie, I said...based on a true story! That's not the worst of it, the little chicken turned out to be a lightweight drinker too! That little spaz started throwing up his Schlitz everywhere! I popped him in his arm as hard as I could and me and my buddies made fun of him a bit! What the hay?...He's my kid brother!

Well, anyhoo, it was pushing midnight, so I figured I'd better be getting him back to the big brother center. I drove the back roads to avoid the cops and promised I'd pick us up some chic's next time. All of a sudden this 'big sister' comes running outside and starts screaming at me about the time for no reason! I winked at Jamboree, to clue him in on the gag, and I grabbed her in a head lock and gave ol' Miss Party Pooper some 'playful' noogies. I figured he'd love it, but no, he starts crying again! So I reached over, gave him atomic wedgie and drove back home!

Man, times sure have changed since I was a kid! I was arrested for assault, DUI, contributing and put on a list banning me from future involvements in any big brother/big sister programs! Whatever, crybabies! Anyhow...after getting paroled last night, I went out and got myself a turtle. I named him Trevor and feed it all the ice cream with sprinkles he can stomach!

Mandy L Cantrell

Mandy L Cantrell is a native of North Georgia who specializes in true to life story telling with a Southern flair. With an honest take on human nature, she weaves a cast of colorful characters through engaging stories that often take a surprising turn. Sometimes happy, often tragic, her stories will engage you with plain spoken, no apologies style writing that lends itself to life's unexpected journeys.

Mandy lives in Calhoun, GA with her husband Heath and their son Johnny. Her education, experience and other interests include: Early childhood education, art, film, photography and outdoor recreation.

Super Chicken and the Wild Bunch
Mandy L Cantrell

About three lots between me and J.W.'s house was a growing side show made up of two trailers and about ten people, best we could tell. In a town with nothing much to do, this had been our favorite attraction during those long summer days. We were still pretty young back then; somewhere between childhood and real responsibility. And we spent most of our time loafing around what was left of a town that may or may not have been something once upon a time.

The group had rolled into town about mid-July in the hottest summer I could ever remember. Days would go by back then with nothing much to do. We'd take long walks up the track and back, maybe ride our bikes down to the creek during the daytime. Nights offered a bunch of T.V. reruns and the same VHSs we'd rented about a hundred times from the gas station.

So when we saw a couple of old junk cars roll into town with more people than car, we decided to check it out. And as the cast of characters filed out of those small vehicles, it didn't take us long to see that something odd was going on.

To most people looking on, things probably seemed pretty normal. After all, it was a small rural town; there was bound to be some people with peculiarities. I mean there was Mrs. Jenkins who always went down to the store with curlers in her hair and for some reason her daughter did the same thing. Then you had John

Stringer's son who had went off to prison last year after he set fire
to the old Creekmore place. Everybody talked about that. Jessie
Bea's cat had a kitten with an extra paw and that was pretty weird.
But there was something more with this bunch. And we wanted to
know what it was.

Our new fascination was a small lot with two singlewides
facing a shared yard that was pretty grown up just a day before. It
was a big group for the space and seemed like a larger head count
every time we went by. Me and J.W. figured it must be a whole
family because we always saw them outside talking and visiting
with each other like they were close knit.

Now the left trailer housed a woman, in what I guessed was
her mid-twenties, and about four kids. Who knows what ailment
kept her from speaking but she sounded as if her tongue had been
cut out. *We said it had been.* She spoke loudly and aggressively
with almost a panic in her cacophony.

We'd walk by or ride our bikes pretending to have some
real destination. And that lady's kids would run out eagerly to
greet us with open arms and bare feet. They looked hardly bathed
and rather excited like so many yard dogs running toward
company.

Me and J.W. would see them on our way to and from the
store just about every time we went down that way (and we went
as much as we could). That unsettled lady would scream at those
kids in a tone that was not startling to them but somewhat
confusing to us. We were never sure if she was encouraging or

discouraging them from talking to us. She was incomprehensive in her constant shriek of vowels.

Across from that distressed woman, lived a man large enough to draw a crowd; the fat man of the side show I presumed. Until curtain call, he was sandwiched in that little place with a woman I took to be his wife, a man they called "Super Chicken" and a plump, little Mexican girl.

Like I said, they weren't quite off target for what you might find around that dead end town except for one thing. To the side of their trailers sat one, rather large, wooden dog house. It could have easily fit two large breeds or, in this case, one large man.

Now the man was not as big as the main attraction, but he was a big guy all the same. From the road you could see him good, overalls and shirtless; a box fan with an orange extension cord stretched outside to cool his humble abode.

On a real hot day, you might see Super Chicken, a wiry, wormy little man in white undershirt and dirty jeans, bullying that big guy with a broom stick while shouting for the man to get back into his cave. Often we heard sounds of frustration and fear as we watched that poor man cower in his wooden box.

Other times we'd catch him in the grass, legs sprawled, resting on the heels of his hands in the bright sunlight just outside his home; a man complacent and somewhat serious, only missing a runner. But he didn't need it. This guy wasn't going anywhere. He didn't even roam the yard.

We noticed that sometimes he just looked like a normal

man, seated on the dry lawn, somewhat bored. Every once in a while they'd bring food out to him and we'd see many of that wild bunch talking in the yard like it was some freak show family reunion.

To add to our curiosity, we noticed that several nights a week an ambulance and fire truck would speed in with lights flashing like the fair! We couldn't figure out why they kept showing up at the trailers. My Momma said something was weird over there and we needed to stay away.

It made her nervous every time we talked about what all we saw there. But we were not afraid. We were not offended by their strange behavior. We were fascinated! In the doldrums of that predictable little town we watched in awe at our new-found attraction. Soaking in the vulgar display and wondering what might come next.

Momma said don't go that way! Don't talk to them! But we did go, we did speak, always hoping they'd invite us into their big tent world but they did not. We were only the audience and must be satisfied with our seating. But their lack of discretion allowed us full admission if only from the road. And we were gonna soak that up no matter how much Momma worried.

Of course the show went on whether we looked or not. They seemed oblivious to the rest of the town. They didn't know they were weird. This was just their normal world. But that curious spread of characters convened every day in the dead heat. Like actors on a stage each one played their own strange part. All we had to do was watch.

But after a while, as much as we enjoyed the show, we couldn't help but wonder *did anybody else think this was weird?* Everyone saw them but no one else was staring. And as far as we knew, nothing was said and nothing was done. Summer days came and went but the man in the doghouse was a constant.

Then one evening me and J.W. were riding our bikes about dusky dark and we glanced eagerly to see who was performing in the yards that Friday night. Unfortunately there was no one outside which was unusual for them. The space was quiet and empty, except for a low hum of the doghouse fan.

Not wanting to miss anything, I suggested we take a closer look while no one was around. We crept alongside the trailers, our hearts beating a little harder, knowing that the whole group was just a few feet away. It was the first time we'd gotten close enough to see behind the curtain and we needed to see the things they hadn't shown us already.

Two more feet and we reached the open window. Inside, a T.V. aired alongside the biggest man of the group who was holding that little Mexican girl up by the throat. I swallowed my gum in one quick gasp and thought for sure I'd choke right there at the open window. Me and J.W. immediately ducked down, hurrying away on bended knees as quickly as we could.

We ran all the way to the pay phone and called the cops. I hung up before they could ask for a name. Within minutes, that now familiar light show flashed through the property once more;

this time induced by our own doing.

We watched from down the street, hoping to see some grand finale. I don't know what all happened inside. But to our surprise, no one left the scene. As far as we knew something strange had been explained and we were left in the dark.

Like all circuses at the end of a season, that wild bunch dwindled out of town not long after that night. Summer brought an early fall and one trailer group at a time settled into a smaller lot on the outskirts of town; someplace along the highway with few houses and less spectators. Who knew what happened there. It was too far to walk.

DB Martin

Best Selling Author, DB Martin - David Brown, was born in Newark New Jersey in 1963. His mother moved to Georgia and he spent his youth in Dalton, Georgia, attending City Park Elementary, Dalton Junior High and Dalton and Ringgold High schools, where he worked on the schools newspapers as an artist, winning many awards. He was also a writer and designer of the annual covers and school mascots, including Georgia's bulldog UGA for Coca-Cola. After graduation he enlisted in the United States Navy, serving his four-year term out of Little Creek Virginia designing military flags. He was then transferred to the USS Hermitage LSD-34, spending most of the time in the Mediterranean Sea and Lebanon during the conflicts there, where he was awarded the Meritorious Service Award and the Presidential Accommodation Medals. After his stent in the military and college he returned to Calhoun, Georgia for a visit where his mother was now residing and during this visit met a local girl name Ellen Fowler, who had just graduated from Calhoun, High school, the beautiful daughter of John and Nancy Fowler who were local residents. He and Ellen were inseparable from the start and have been since they married in 1985. They had a daughter Megan who they lost not long after birth, then their son Joshua David Lee Brown was born in 1988, a musician who currently resides in Brooklyn, NY. After getting married, David quickly established himself as a writer, illustrator and designer. His story published in 1982 called Bedtime for Sam, has been critically acclaimed and used in numerous movies and television shows. David currently is an award winning rug designer and display designer. He writes and illustrates for many magazines and digests under several pen names and does professional design work for many of the fortune 500 companies. He writes and is an author of many genres (fiction novels, Horror, Poetry Books, Children's stories and books, and odd stories for many magazines).

David and his wife Ellen currently reside in Georgia. He is an active Member of the Georgia Writer's association, Calhoun Area Writers and The Dalton Area Writers.

Truth
DB Martin

The hordes they often come
And gather all around
They look at me quite bewildered
Not making any sound

Then one alone inquires
As all eyes do lift and stare
Waiting for the answer
Anticipation in the air

The question itself an old one
Answered so long ago
And the answer it is easy
And it's an answer they should know.

For when they see the eyes of children
And the wonder that is there
When they see the ocean ebbing
When they stop and breathe the air

When they see the morning sun
And the rain upon the land
When they hear a kittens purr
And when a child takes them by the hand

When the flowers bloom in the springtime
And trees turn in fall
When snow falls white upon the world
And they are there for it all

When they watch the world evolving
Growing as it should
When they see the forest trees
And they see that it is good

When they watch a waterfall
Cutting through the land
Feeding life throughout the world
Just as it was planned

When they see a sunsets glow
And fish swimming in the sea
When they meet that special one
And they know it's meant to be

Why they cannot see
What they know is really there
Either they're blind to the world
Or simply just don't care

For the answer is quite simple
But the question I find odd.
Because of course the answers, yes
Yes, there is a God.

Christmas Tears
DB Martin

On a patch of ground, in the center of a wood,
Alone in the moonlight, a small tree stood.

Bending its branches over toward the ground,
And in the cracks of its bark, tears could be found.

And a weeping could be heard all through the wood,
A sad kind of sound and sad is not good.

Then out of a door, built in a dirt mound,
A Newbling child came, from in under the ground.

Slowly he walked up to the sad tree and smiled,
"Why are you sad little tree, why?" said the child.

And the little tree not knowing at all what to say,
Said, "Why, why nothing is wrong, I'm quite fine today."

"It's so nice of you to care, and it's really quite kind,
Thank you for asking but, but really I'm fine."

"Little tree," said the child "please don't be sad,
For tomorrow is Christmas, oh and it's a time to be glad."

"How anyone can be sad on Christmas, really I don't know,
With all those presents under the tree, tied up with big bows."

"With lights twinkling and family home from afar,
Oh! And the stories, the stories, of the great Christmas star."

"How the wise men followed the star in the sky,

And how it shined higher than any on high."

"How the angels came down, to the shepherd and their sheep,
And told them of the place, where God's child lay asleep."

"How the baby born in a stable that night,
Would grow to a man, who stood for what was right."

"Not a nobler man could have been sent here to lead,
Oh! What a wonderful and joyous night indeed."

With that, the little tree again began to cry,
And the Newbling child still did not know why,

"Please tell me little tree, why it is that you have cried?"

"Because I know the story," said the tree, "of how that child died."

Final Words
DB Martin

As I sit here with quill in hand,
Under the gaslights amber glow.
I scratch upon the paper,
As the narrative, it does flow.

Like blood from a wound,
It feeds the quill.
As I scribe the pages,
Without thought or will.

They come like memories,
Though memories not.
From a dark imagination,
That only Hell begot.

I question the sanity,
That pens these words.
That flow from within,
In hellish herds.

Frightful tales,
That chill the soul.
As Imagery and reverie,
Take control.

As letters form words,
And words become tales.
Do they truly show me?
Do they expose beneath the veils?

Or do they simply represent,
Imagination and heart.
Some twisted and perverted form,
Of what we call art.

Heaven's Rain
DB Martin

I ran and ran, out into the night,
Just as the darkness, faded into light.

And came to a place, where the land did peak,
And I raised my eyes, to the skies to speak.

And asked my lord, to save my soul,
To remove the evil, to make me whole.

And I asked, why this he allowed,
When in his words, love was vowed.

Then a breeze began, down soft and low,
And quickly grew, into a daunting blow.

Heaven's fire pushed and pulled the wind,
As clouds and sky together blend.

A mass of grays and blacks do fold,
And thunder trilled, as it severely scold.

And the vision faded from my eyes,
As darkness grew and the light it dies.

And I stood alone in consternation,
A witness to this, God's creation.

No shelter held me to its breast,
Alone facing what I could not contest.

Then rain came down in torrents screaming,
Though no lights, the sheets were gleaming.

Like razors cutting within my skin,
I dared raise my eyes and shout again.

"What evil did I do to this be caused?"
And with these words the storm it paused.

And a light broke through the dark beyond,
From he, whom this storm had spawned.

And shown down upon a simple child,
Myself, who stood alone beguiled.

And a voice rang down bold and true,
"Who doubts my choice, my child, you?"

"A doubt my lord, never nay,
But merely a question did I convey."

"A prayer I asked, and a question too.
 Should a question be asked? I ask of you."

Then lightning cracked, and thunder roared,
I feared that I had upset the lord.

The skies again, drew open wide,
And heaven's rain fell from deep inside.

And it tore the ground from with under,
Pulling me down, down asunder.

Clawing, reaching, for some ground.

But nothing stable could be found.

"Lord," I screamed again, "what have I done?
That you would punish me, your son."

Then the thunder ceased, and the lightening staid,
And light shown through, as the darkness fade.

Then a hand lift me, and lay me on the ground,
As I knelt there before, the one who's crowned.

Then the voice thundered down from the lamb,
"You dared to question, the great I am."

How I trembled, words lost within my fear
My eyes casting down dropped a tear.

Then a light shown, from the above
Through the darkness, he spoke of love

See me, child, see me as I am,
And hear the bleating of the lamb.

My reasons you may not comprehend
with vanity, you feel that you alone, do fend

The thunder child, and the rain I send,
The gentle breeze, the twisting wind,

The things I do and have done,
Even the fires from the sun.

I do not care for my child, for who,
For what I do, is for all of you.

For in my heart there is only love,
For you are my children and I the dove.

Inside
DB Martin

In the obscurity, I was awoken,
Torn from my slumber.
A noise of some uncertainty,
The world sewn in umber.

My posture it ascended,
As I devoured every sound.
The desire for review abstained,
As hysteria abound.

Then blustering above the silence,
There further came discord.
As I wade across my harbor,
And placed my foot upon the board.

Then I rose within the dimness,
Drapery is drawn.
Dawned only in a vestment,
My legs embracing the chiffon.

Shifts of agitation,
Still, emanate from below.
Vibrations with repetition.
Like the pecking of a crow.

As I traverse my chambers goods,
And made my way unto the door.
There below came a calling,
As it rang out again, again once more.

Within my hand, I held the latch,

That freed me from discord.
Though curiosities attention,
Caused reason to be ignored,

The latch like a thorn,
It burn with my palm.
As violent thoughts entered in,
And forced away the calm.

It rolled within my hand,
And opened up the shore.
And as I stared between the wood,
The eddy pulled me through the door.

Now within the gallery,
I stood naked and exposed.
Unclear where to go and move,
With the route behind me closed.

My meager gait shifted forward,
As faces stare from walls.
My interest turns to fear,
As I walk these lonely halls.

I held my breath,
As my heart kept the time.
Slowly, slowing down,
As the clock did chime.

Hollow echoes down the hall,
Cause shivers to ignite.
As the tattler screams out to all,
The hour is midnight.

I stood atop the staircase,
Gazing down the avenue.
As my head began to swim,
And steps they went askew.

Then again the agitation,
Rising from below.
Broke the airs frenzy,
And again clarity was bestow.

Slowly I descended,
Cascading down the grade.
Listening to the air,
As the sounds, they do fade.

Gazing to the left and right,
Hoping not to see.
What I feared within my heart,
And knew what would be.

Then once again is heard,
The voices of unrest.
Causing my heart to distend,
And I pause to clutch my breast.

Then a deluge of fear befalls,
As a shadow comes to light.
And I reverse to ascend,
Swiftly up the flight.

 Abaft the invader's shadow,
Reaches toward the stair.
And pauses for a moment,
When it finds no one is there.

I abscond across the gallery,
Unto my chamber door.
And nimbly I enter in,
And lay upon the floor.

Then I crawl beneath my harbor,
And lay without a sound.
And I listened quite intently,
As my tension comes unwound.
 Then I heard upon the landing,
Like nothing heard before.
Something shifting, someone stirring,
Right outside my chamber door.

I retained my screams deep inside,
In the stillness, I remained.
Held beneath of my own accord.
Now harnessed and chained.

 My body became taut,
As I lay in agony.
Attempting to be silent,
But it was just not to be.

It started rather low,
Then it grew within my ear.
The beating of my heart so loud,
So loud that I could hear.

I feared within my mind,
That the beating was so strong.
That the shadow it could hear it,
And I wouldn't be hiding very long.

Then a breath rushed down my spine,
As my door swung slowly free.
Leave me please I thought inside,
Go and let me be.

Then tears began to flow,
As I lay and held my breath.
As I beseeched God within my hold,
From this beast, I knew as death.

  Then the shadow moved before me,
It ran across my chamber floor.
No longer was my harbor safe,
As the storm approach the shore.
 The shadow flowed across the board,
As fears inertia held me fast.
Then it moved back to the door,
Safety at last.

Then it turned, and it stormed upon me,
And grasp about my leg.
And pulled me from my harbor,
As I began to scream and beg.

Then within the darkness of my chamber,
The shadow became flesh.
As I kicked and I screamed,
And I flailed, and I thresh.

Now free within the room,
He held me to the floor.
Screaming out profanities,
Of what he held in store.

I was simply overpowered,
As I lay within the dark,
As he tore away my innocence,
And laughed there in the dark.

But I never stopped protesting,
So I never let him win,
And I never left that spot
And I never will again.

Sorrow
DB Martin

Between branches black and withered,
lay the darkened pools of sorrow.
Laden in spores of absinthe moss,
to never see tomorrow.

Never to see the rays of the sun,
to know daylight from the dark.
For sorrow lives in darkness,
between the blackened cracks of bark

For when those we love do go,
and life it yellows and dies.
Tears are shed from those who loved,
tears from sorrows eyes.

Eyes that once knew happiness,
and now lay it on the cross.
They cry those bitter tears,
and damn God for their loss.

They cast denunciation.
They point and place the blame.
And do not thank the lord,
for the love that they did claim.

They only see the loss,
not the fortune that they held.
They look only forward,
And not at what life itself expelled.

So for every tear that falls,

and feeds the stagnant pools.
That lie within the branches,
are the shallow tears of fools.

Michael Zemaitis

Michael Zemaitis has been a grave digger, scrapper, professor, and an electronics computer expert for the Department of Homeland Security.

He survived combat in Vietnam with the NAVY. He also survived kickboxing 2 rounds with a world champion. He always states, "How many lives am I given to survive?"

From dancing ZUMBA with his female friends, gardening, and aging like the wine he makes, he shares the breadth and depth of his life giving a poignant insight to the world that he traveled. Michael was published in USA Today, Phillies Report, and many magazines that deal with the electronic and computer engineering. He currently writes short stories for his audience.

Do You Believe in Miracles?
Michael Zemaitis

How many Christian's are in this world? A billion? More?

Most of them have read parts of the Bible and do know the story of Jesus' birth and His life on earth. The Bible also mentions many miracles in the Old and the New Testaments. Making oil last for many days, trumpets blowing down the walls, swallowed by a whale and still alive. Then turning water into wine, healing the sick, multiplying food, walking on water, and raising the dead. That was a long, long time ago.

Do we ever see miracles? Are they real or just hoaxes performed on television to get our money? Are the people that are healed in a hysterical state of mind that hypnotic strange words can make them feel better? Or are they shills planted in the audience like butter on popcorn?

The Catholic Church demands miracles for people nominated to be canonized into sainthood. They must have three miracles for sainthood. The name of the person up for sainthood should be mentioned in the prayers to God asking for the miracles. I often wonder if they film these actual events or do they wait for people that have "miraculous" rejections of cancer, disease, or neurological disorders walk in to the Pope and say, "I am better because of this person named Fred that God want's to be a saint".

I don't know.

For me the proof that there are miracles came to me from my

sister and her husband. Mary Ann and Tom were the perfect match and the best partners and friends a marriage could create. They loved, laughed, cried, argued and created. Just like you and me. Two sons were their only offspring. They too grew up and had families of their own. Life was good and fulfilling.

We are all mortals and parts of us break down. In Mary Ann and Tom's case the beginning of the end of this fairy tale romance was Tom developing prostate cancer. In his case many diagnoses and other conditions interfered with him getting early life saving treatment.

Tom went to a doctor early on and complained about erectile dysfunction. His doctor gave him a rectal exam that detected no "lumps". Viagra was then a new drug that doctors gave out willingly and he was given a prescription to see if the drug would help him get over the hump.

Tom was also a corporate manager and was always flying across the United States and to Europe to fulfill the requirements of his job. The time and places for him to get together with his wife were infrequent and usually planned ahead of time for a dinner party or a weekend with the grandchildren. I smile whenever I see the commercial for Cialis with a man and a woman in separate bath tubs. The time and place aren't always just right.

The Viagra had no effect so a frustrated Tom went back to the doctor. The warning signs were there, they were misread, and cell by cell his body was multiplying this cancer deep inside.

This time when Tom went back to his doctor they decided to

do a PSA test. The results were an 11. Anything above a two is deemed strategically iffy. Above 5 the situation can be a requirement for more tests, but above 10 was almost proof positive he had prostate cancer.

The doctors involved with cancer of this type talked with Tom and Mary Ann about their options for dealing with the disease. They both agreed to attack it head on when the doctors in his cancer treatment center found that Tom had blockages in arteries in his neck.

"We can't do any radiation treatment until his blood flow is back to normal." This dilemma set back the radiation treatment that was planned to burn the cancer in the body. The cells multiplied and multiplied. What may seem a small area of cancer in reality is a vicious package of the body turning itself inside out.

Tom had stints inserted in his neck arteries and recovered enough blood flow so that his treatment could begin. Tests were given to find the root, and he was then tattooed so the radiologist always had the same target. Day by day he was radiated at the source. The treatment is tiring and soon becomes deadly. X-ray beams are shot and focused into the body to burn the problem area, but they are also going through healthy tissue. Tom would vomit often and was losing his taste for food. But he survived the 16 week process.

The doctors told Tom and Mary Ann that this was a "stop gap" measure. They were informed that his PSA would be close to zero after radiation; however the case was so advanced that they said Tom would require chemotherapy sometime in the future. They also told Tom that he would need transfusions, but that wouldn't be a problem because Tom had donated 10 gallons of his own blood throughout his life to save others.

I never knew what my sister and Tom discussed about the future. There had to be hundreds of issues dealing with insurance, their sons, their grandchildren and whatever we can think about when we know the end is coming within a known time frame. One thing my sister did insist to Tom is that when he died, she wanted immediate proof that his soul was out of his body and that he was off to somewhere better.

The countdown of weeks, months and the first year flew by. Tom's PSA did diminish, and for a while it was normal. Then one day the weekly PSA level jumped to 3 from near zero and the next stage of treatment began.

Chemotherapy is essentially putting specific poisons in the body to try to abate the progress of the cancer. Many are from natural products like the yew bush or the mandrake root. Others are synthetically designed to attack only one type of cell as like a guided missile. The worst problem with the treatment is that the poison is poisoning everything good and bad at the same time. The only recompense is that in developing these poisons, researchers found that the good wasn't destroyed enough not to survive and live again.

This is where the transfusions take place. Blood caries nourishment, oxygen, and waste through our body. The blood is also affected by the poison. In order to survive you need fresh blood.

This process of treatment, transfusion, rest went on for several months. Tom could still enjoy life and do almost anything he wished. The only thing he noticed was the lethargy and weakness caused by his illness.

One day in September my sister called me, "Tom fell and I can't get him up."

"I'm on my way."

Tom was sitting on the floor looking confused. He had a little smile on his face as he said, "Whoops, I didn't see that coming."

Mary Ann and I got him in a chair and she called the prearranged hospice care. Tom wanted to die in his own home looking over the east brow of Lookout Mountain.

When the hospice workers came with the hospital bed I went home to pack some belongings and came back to be with my sister and Tom.

The end comes quicker than the beginning. Tom was in a coma only 2 hours later. One son was able to be there with his mother because of the suddenness of the situation. The other son was out of state on vacation.

We took turns holding his hand, tried to give him ice chips, and watched as his breathing became slower and slower. Then the death rattles began. I am told that these are the last gasps into the congested lungs.

Tom seemed very uncomfortable and I injected a sedative into the IV in his arm. If anything, it stirred him more and his last breath left.

In a blink he was gone and in a blink the alarm system began wailing in the house. We all jumped up to see if there was any cause or way to turn it off. For about twenty seconds it wailed, and then stopped.

I looked at my nephew, and then at my sister. She was crying, moaning, and had a smile on her face all at once.

"Thank you Tom, thank you God, thank you."

The miracle was complete.

Weeks later I had the alarm people come out and check the system. I mentioned to the technicians that it hadn't been checked in several years due to Tom suffering from cancer. I said that I wanted to be sure my sister had some protection as she began her journey forward without her husband. The technician took time and more time to test every window sensor, door sensor, smoke sensor, carbon monoxide sensor as well as the optical sensors that set off the alarm if anything passed by in front of them.

"There's nothing wrong with this system," said the technician, "even the backup battery is fully charged."

I knew this was going to be the result. Somehow, some way, Tom had found a way to let Mary Ann know that his life wasn't in vain. He proved in his last instant in this mortal plane that we are all moving onward to a new existence.

Jan Deems

Jan Deems has been writing in journals since her adolescent years. She found journaling was way to go back and learn from her past. As an adult Christian writer, she wrote inspirational articles for her church monthly newsletter. She began seriously writing in 2009 as she had a passion for what was happening in America. She has written numerous articles regarding the only way to put our country back on track was to put God back in America. She was a co-founder of a Tea Party in her community where she would always start the meeting with an article she had written regarding how America can learn how to correct its mistakes by studying scripture; learning through our biblical ancestors sin of turning from God and how it affected not just them but their entire nation. She also had written a political blog on getting America back to its grassroots. Jan is Christian, teaches adult Sunday school and continues to write Christian true-life experiences in a short story inspirational format. She is now concentrating on her first book.

What Does it Matter to America Anyway?
Jan Deems

My foremost passion, like most everyone else is for the welfare of my children and grandchildren. Secondly, I have an ongoing passion to bring God back into America where He belongs.

What we do today – matters greatly to future generations of Americans. There are millions of Americans who have been praying because they are enormously concerned about the condition of our country. Anyone who studies history will tell you that history does repeat itself. Therefore, it is imperative we look back – way back – to biblical times.

There is a wealth of information to study and learn from as we look into the mistakes of our biblical ancestors. This is important to do because America is now making some of the same mistakes resulting in an increase in the depravity of humanity. We can look at what happened to Israel and investigate how we can apply that lesson to our country because while Americans are not God's chosen people, we are a nation which was founded on God. We need to turn this great country of ours back into the godly foundation it was built. And we can only do that through on God.

One of America's main problems is caused by many of our self-serving politicians *on both sides of the fence*, that is, Democrats and Republicans whose greed and self-serving attitudes have increasingly become more important than the welfare of future generations of America. For instance, what have they done to eliminate our national deficit which now totals the trillions of dollars? *Nothing*. What many of them do care about is lining their pockets. There are some godly men and women who have been elected to Congress who to abide by and defend our Constitution. While they are a minority, they are strong because God is with and for them in their quest to turn America back to its grassroots.

The corruption and sin of the people of the Israel nation, and how it led to them being taken from their own country and placed into captivity in another land *is something we absolutely need to learn from*. We do not have time to waste. We need to search out and comprehend that America's congress is jam-packed with the corruption of greed, deceit and immoral behavior which parallels the depravity of our biblical ancestors.

The Israelites, because of their sin, lived in exile in Babylon for over seventy years. We need to consider that many of our leaders are just as bad, if not more so, than the Israelites. We have some in Congress who are trying to turn our democracy (and our freedom) into a socialistic government. It has been happening because "We the People" *who are suppose to be in charge* have sat back and basically allowed their turncoat actions. What they have done to this country is deplorable. Their sin has not only produced the current condition of our country but our children and grandchildren's lives will also be greatly affected by their actions. God will not only hold them accountable for their corruption but He will also hold the people of America accountable because we have sat on our comfortable couches while allowing their self-centered greed to prosper.

Let's take a look back into history and see how we can apply that to America today some 3000 years later. As we delve into this portion of scripture (2 Kings 18-20), we find there were some leaders back then who were also corrupt and didn't care about the people either; it was all about them. One is a king by the name of Hezekiah. He was basically a good king *until he felt that whiff of power which steadily grew within him* until one day he said, in effect the same mantra of today, "What does it matter anyway?"

In response to being asked at a congressional hearing about the American men and women who died in Benghazi, Hillary Clinton responded "What does it matter now anyway?" This philosophy, unfortunately, has been fueled by many of our congressional leaders. They have made it all about them when our Constitution clearly states *they were elected to serve the America people*.

King Hezekiah, if alive today, would probably *lean toward* the conservative side of the equation. Basically, he did everything right in the eyes of the Lord even tearing down the false idols people worshipped. *"He trusted God… no one like him… faithful in everything and carefully obeyed"[1]*. He really had it going on until he made the mistake of allowing his pride and the aroma of power to become his pilot; thus, *through his own greed, he was in the race for more* – always more. Sounds like many of our politicians, doesn't it? One little hint of clout intertwined with control and suddenly it is all about them instead of our country and the people in it.

Hezekiah became gravely ill and the prophet Isaiah told him that he was going to die. Hezekiah on hearing the news of his impending death became very bitter. Because he felt he had been a good king who followed after God, he asked God that he would not die and wept bitterly. One thing important to note in reading this scripture is that Hezekiah completely *understood that God had allowed this illness because of his pride*; however, *"...Hezekiah gave not return for the benefit he received because his heart was proud."*[2]

Due to his immense wealth, Hezekiah's heart was already proud before he became ill. However, God gave him a second chance and extended his life. In that, you would think Hezekiah would have been grateful but he wasn't. Instead, we observe a further glimpse of his increasingly proud attitude when God told him he would give him a choice (as a sign of healing) that the shadow in the stairway would either go forward or backward an additional ten steps. Hezekiah's response is very telling of his arrogance. He said *"it is easy for the shadow to decline ten steps; no, let the shadow turn backward ten steps."*[3] In his self-importance, he probably ascertained that as King, "the sign" should not be something effortless but something more demanding which would be fitting of a man in his position. It would be like watching a sundial at 1:00 which would normally go from 1:00 to

1:10, but instead, would go from 1:00 to 12:50.

God allowed Hezekiah's sickness to show him his sin of pride. However, Hezekiah did not learn the lesson. After God healed him, ambassadors *from the evil nation of Babylon* came calling on Hezekiah who, with an inflated ego, showed them *everything* in his kingdom. We can compare it to an American president ld allowing evil forces to see within the operational secrets of something like Homeland Security. We might stop here and ask ourselves, would an *actual* American president do that? Hezekiah, in essence, did show the enemy everything. Then the prophet of God, Isaiah, told him a day was coming when *all that you have will be taken* from you and carried off to Babylon.

The parallel of this to America today is important. Hezekiah had *allowed the enemy* in and *freely showed them everything* so God *allowed that enemy to destroy* Hezekiah's kingdom and all that was in it. We need to first note that the destruction of that nation *began* under Hezekiah's rule. Even more critical to mention is those who would suffer the effects of his sin. It would be his sons; the kingdom would be taken from his sons. Fast forward to today. We have not been standing up for America and what it stands for. Evil has infiltrated our country and it continues to get worse.

Why did this happen? This is the "sixty-four thousand dollar" question and the answer is in scripture. When Hezekiah *was told it would be his children who would be most affected* by his sin, Hezekiah had the audacity to basically say "*well that is good; it won't happen to me but to my children*"[4]   In his self-centered arrogant world, he was only concerned about what happened to himself not his children or the kingdom. No matter which way you look at it, sin is evil. Case in point: our children and grandchildren are going to inherit and will have to deal with a national deficit that was not of their making.

That is exactly what has been happening to our country as our past president, aided by many people in Congress, laid the kindling of embracing the enemy not only within our government but also by opening our borders to anyone without any manner of censorship. You can take this to the bank: *nothing escapes God notice*. What has been done through immoral congressmen is clearly not just only against our Constitution but against God because America was founded on "In God We Trust". Eventually there is going to be a heavy price to be paid and like Israel, if we don't start voting and weeding out the bad we will be like Israel *and it will cost Americans our freedom*!

Judgment, as a result of our sin, has already come upon America. We have been ingrained with a political correctness agenda which basically calls "good" evil and calls "evil" good. Right now we are holding off losing the country we grew up in only because millions of concerned Americans have been praying and fasting. I feel sure we now have a president who believes in God and is doing everything he can to restore America. He continues to do exactly what he said he would do before being elected. He is 100% for our Constitution, America and the people within and he deeply needs our prayers. I believe many of the "fat-cats" in Washington, D.C. now realize the "jig is up" and not only will their corruption be exposed but their overweight paychecks will be going "bye-bye" and they are doing everything they can to fight against it.

It is time we started standing up for America and the foundation it was built on. We can start by voting out the bad and, if need be, take them out of office by petition. I do not want to see my grandchildren living under socialism where a person has no freedom.

Cuba, unfortunately is a good example of life without freedom. If living under the control of a government is so great, why are so many citizens of that country trying to escape from living there? Did you note that "escape" part? *They are not allowed to leave; they must escape.* There are only two levels of social order there: the few super wealthy and then the vast majority of the population who live in poverty with no way out. That is one of the main reasons so many people want to come to America to live. If you work hard, you can progress out of it.

I end with this. "God, please bring a heavy revival upon our country; it will only be by Your hand that America can be brought back to the nation our forefathers fought so hard for. We need and want to return to "In God – and God alone - We Trust". Amen

1- 2 Kings 18:5; [2]- 2 Chronicles 32:25; [3]- 2 Kings 20:9; [4]- 2 Kings 20:16-17; [5]- 2 Kings 20:19

94817917R00107

Made in the USA
Columbia, SC
07 May 2018